I0474947

PUSHING ROCKS **DOWN**HILL

EMPOWERING THE RELATIONSHPS IN BUSINESS: EMPLOYEES, CUSTOMERS
AND MYSELF

Michael Kliman

INTRODUCTION

Why do we work? With more than one half of our waking hours devoted to this purpose, the answer to the question must satisfy more than financial arithmetic.

For sure we work for the money, and without it most of us would never be inclined or able to donate the time. If one thing is clear to me, cash may be said to king, but at best it is a lesser monarch, a conditioned reinforcer, if you will. When people acquire enough of it inevitably they choose to exercise their discovered freedom to abandon work to devote themselves to what it is they really do want to do. It is called *work* for a reason. Thus, *time* is the actual reigning king.

The fact of money actually NOT being the end all but the means to it, suggests the presence of other motivations that are at least important and maybe even more appealing than the bucks themselves. In fact, I have observed the vital role in myself and in employees of some of these unspoken needs. I would go declaratively further to propose that it is the subtle nourishing of these alternative impulses that is the very driver of professional satisfaction, professional performance and professional commitment. It is the necessary condition for achieving the business metaphor of business performance as the proverbial engine firing on all cylinders, with a fully functioning professional being one who uses the totality of his/her personal talents with *commitment* and *enthusiasm*.

Peak performance, being in the zone, full functioning are not mere concepts, but actual modes of being. This does not happen casually and most of us would wait forever for it to happen. As the employer, it is imperative for me to discover what I can do to promote this in my help. It then serves my bottom-line interest to work like crazy to provide these conditions to bring the help to a closer approximation of that ideal performance level than would just happen without my input.

PEAK PERFORMANCE, IN THE ZONE:
If I don't work to make it happen, who will?
If I don't work to make it happen can I expect it?

I recognize in myself the operation of pride, the need for recognition and belonging, and various other personality desires. None of these would carry the same weight without the catalyst of income, but I have observed the direct relationship of the satisfaction of these to MY attitude and performance. By exercising even just a little sensitivity I unavoidably make the same recognition in my employees. These observations have led to an easy conclusion that it benefits me and my business goals to strive to arrange for the satisfaction of all of my employees' needs in order to maximize their performance, i.e. *maximize my profit.*

How is this done?

A worker who feels good about himself will perform better. A worker who is well paid, has opportunity to earn more, receives bonus incentives, feels accepted, cared for and respected will clearly work better. This is the goal of EVERY employer. And it is *worth* working for. It is the most important function of a service/ trades work employer.

Customers are not different in this regard. Although their primary motivation is a job well done and on time, they also have THEIR ego needs. Any service provider who likes to get paid upon finishing their job had better cater to these needs or suffer the consequences of a benefactor's unmet expectations.

I have, then, identified two types of relationships in business: with employees and with customers. To complete the round table of relationships I consider relationship with myself.

Mindfulness is not just a buzz word of flavor of the month business or therapeutic fad, but an ancient practice of spiritual development. To my understanding, it is essentially an effort of honest, complete, sincere and ever penetrating awareness. What about these characteristics does NOT apply to business performance?

PUSHING ROCKS DOWNHILL

The more complete my awareness, in sincerity, honesty and penetration, the greater is the foundation of data I act upon. This is even Simple Science 101. The more facts I have, the greater is my ability to predict and manage my science experiment. In this case I am a behavioral scientist, and it behooves me to observe and understand all of the motivating factors of the people involved in this endeavor: my employees, my customers and myself.

To overlook what I am able to observe would be *numb and dumb*. Therefore I must go out of my way to practice mindfulness of myself, others and all of the circumstances. The more and better I do this the more it benefits my business goals.

The crux of my outlook is to bring the greatest concentration of attention to that upon which I will have the greatest amount of control. This means I will place ultimate responsibility on myself, looking to myself as being where conscious management of behavior can take place. The buck will not only stop with me, but start with me as well. I am the one whose behavior I can control. My partners in business relationship, employees and customers, will respond to how I am. My goal is to maximize my attention for the relevant behavioral factors which will maximize my business partners' participation, but the only one whose behavior I can directly control is mine.

All of my motivations rest upon the fact that I want to be kind and considerate to the people in my life. In business, I still have this but with *a goal orientation*.

I do not analyze, categorize or pigeon hole anyone. What I want is to maximize my goals by maximizing the engagement of business partners' willing participation in the joint experiment in which we are engaged. I place the greatest burden on myself to act correctly, as the engine that drives the rest of the train.

How can I act when talking to a prospect? What kind of person does it take to handle a critical customer? What can I do in myself when I try to sell a job?

Who in me is there who knows how to ask a stranger for a job? Is there one in me who can have confidence in the face of diversity?

What is my relationship to these guys? Who am I to them? How can I get more out of them? How do I gain their trust? What would it mean to be trustworthy?

Some books will tell you all about other people. They will tell you how they are and what they do. They will go on about how you break them up into categories and subcategories, and then all about the character traits of each of them. They will tell you everything you need to know about others so that you will know what to expect FROM THEM. What to expect from the other is not the focus of this book or my business and especially not my life. My focus has been about what to expect FROM ME, how to find and release in myself what I need so that I can maximize what I need from others.

My life has been to understand what I can do in a world of me who is with all of you. This is how I have considered myself in arriving at what I want from you.

Michael Kliman
March 2011

SUFI WISDOM:

trust in God,
but tie up your camel

CONTENTS

PART 1: THE BEGINNING

ME

I've not always been a house painter. Nor am I always now, either, for that matter. My inner self changes with my pursuits, and it has certainly changed with the times of my life.

Whereas in my earlier professional career I was a supportive and care giving psychologist treating severely dysfunctional children, I am now a profit-oriented, bottom-line type of guy. These two sides of me seemingly don't go together, but interestingly at this stage of my life and career, they sit side by side, and acting in unison as each expresses itself in a dance of a more complete self-expression.

I was trained in the Establishment and Modification of Behavior. I was an expert in Behavior Management, and I was quite good at my skills of working with handicapped kids. In a broader sense of my training, I was a communication and training pro. And it was this particular take on what I did that became the basis for my style of relationship to employees.

All of my dealings with the men of my many crews were put into the framework of a behavior analyst's viewpoint: setting-behavior - consequence. I was quite disciplined with myself in using the principles I had used so well to establish and modify the behavior of under- functioning children with the guys working for me. And though my relationship with them on the surface was not on the same level of life change that my work with kids was, I have always had the feeling I was providing more of a vocational rehabilitation environment for those guys than an ordinary employment situation.

Of course, I was running a business and therefore had to make money. Truth be told: I never liked painting, hated it as a kid, and

1

So the only sense to be made from the painting business was to do something interesting with it and to do well with income.

I have been doing this "summer job" now for thirty years, and enjoy more time off, travel and hobby pursuits than anyone I know who must work for a living. When I'm asked, I will say I am a college kid with a summer job...except I quit college. My typical year consists of six to seven months of business and five to six months of personal pursuit. I think of it as taking my retirement half a year at a time. I call this not a bad schedule.

I especially like it during the winter when I ski three or four times a week at home, take one of my two or three annual ski trips or take an adventure travel trip to places such as Israel or Nepal. I especially like this schedule when I can take six months to pursue a writing project, or two months to remodel my house. And sometimes I just read, putter, and in no way impose a schedule on myself. I don't like it as much from April through November, though.

The pursuits and mood of my day take a 180* turn during the season of business hours. When the painting season bell rings, I am out of the gate like a race horse and don't look back until fall. The self of me that knows the lifestyle of temporary retirement goes to sleep, the world-beater comes crashingly awake and the world is filled with painting, business concerns, schedules and problems to solve.

This guy is driven, ambitious and aggressive. It is so busy my retired side must sleep through it. These two shouldn't co-exist. Although I believe the one exists to provide relief for the other. If not for the other, either one would become predominant, most likely stale and, worst of all, fixed in me.

I see so many burned-out business people. I see burned-out, jaded ski bums as well. When a life has a sole focus, the person becomes a one-trick pony. He only does one thing and that without opposition. I value my balanced life of opposite pursuits. For me, the coin is neither just heads nor just tails, but, obviously, both.

I have been following this schedule for thirty years. At various times I have referred to it as farming or harvesting, or even squirreling. There is a productive period wherein I must earn, and this is followed by a temporary retirement that might last as long as the harvesting period. Eventually, my half and half lifestyle emerged and developed into the opposites I know now.

It was really only recently that I came to a realization that this yearly cycle is an annual achievement, requiring skill and hard work, about which I ought to be proud. I admit that there has been not a little sheepishness in me when the subject of my time off would appear as the topic of conversation. It has not been the case that I have expressed self-satisfaction in having achieved my winter of Saturdays. But instead I have felt in some way apologetic for all of this free time; not with an understanding of my having earned it, but rather I seemed to have felt it was some kind of unearned vacation. This attitude had spread the rumor in me that my life had granted me unearned time off and, somewhere in me, I believed I didn't deserve it. Now, my winter of Saturdays is the very goal that justifies the whole enterprise.

As for my business life, I do it because of the income, for the income. I've learned to do it well and I have risen to the top of my profession. I have said for years that the painting trade is made up of misfits, drifters and bums, including employers as well as their employees. That to distinguish one's self in this business is like my being tall at a nursery school: merely stand up and be erect. Looking good in this crowd isn't really all that demanding.

I constantly remind my crew that we are not in the painting business, or even just *merely* the painting business. Rather, we are in the Show Business, offering the Painting Show. If you put on a good show, people enjoy the production and pay the price willingly. If you put on a bad show, they don't. I put on a good show. People pay and they tell their friends. It seems to work out. And when I am done for the year, I get a winter of Saturdays.

So I have engaged this little research and development project of mine from a totally new perspective than the ordinary tradesman. In this, the trade itself has been secondary to the training and management aspects of my employee relationships. My customer relations have been guided by an enlightened sense of openness and complete disclosure. The upshot has been a highly successful, small trade's service business

If it is true that we must learn from our experience that is not always what happens. Whereas one can have thirty years' experience with some endeavor, it can as easily be one year's experience thirty times as it could be thirty years of new experiences. It also is true that we are creatures of habit, a self-imposed master who drives us to do and repeat the same procedures over and over. The requirement to learn then is in a sense antithetical to getting things done. In my haste to get things done I made my share of mistakes early on, and they cost me plenty. They cost me, but the expense represents payment for education received. And the lessons learned form the basis for who I am as a business man and how I do it.

Interestingly, however smart I thought I was when I began proved to be nowhere near smart enough. Sure, I had my college and graduate level education, including a Bachelor's degree, two Masters and PhD training, but my sequestered, privileged, Ivy League type life was no preparation for the business exchange of life.

Think about the crafty middle- eastern shop owner whose negotiating skill fleeces even the worldliest traveler. Think about the cliché absent-minded professor who forgets his most essential item. I was book smart but street dumb. And boy, did I take a lickin'!

At the end of thirty-plus years of this exercise I value my business experience on a par with or even above my academic education. There is something quite real about business experience and the entrepreneurial spirit. But the real truth of this attitude plays itself out not just in doing the business, but in living one's life as well.

In myself, I find certain undeniable changes. Gone are conventions. Gone is being less than anyone. Gone is the need to wait to be told it is my turn. Gone is playing second fiddle. In the place of all that playing by the rules "they" have given us is making up my own rules. The personal empowerment that comes from starting, running and succeeding at one's own business is all-consuming. The world is my playground; the people in it are no more than my peers. No one is my superior. And wherever I go I am at the top of the food chain.

When I started, though, a "high pressure *system*" of my ideas and beliefs was confronted by a "cold front" of hard fact of truth. The reality storm that broke out became my revered teacher. Like it or not, I was compelled to accept that truth was what was happening. It wasn't what I believed ought to happen. And I reluctantly, if valuably, took my education as the bitter pill it was. I paid. And I learned as I went.

THE THREE LESSONS

Call me anal, but I've always been a person who hates unfinished tasks and loose ends. I hate it when the dishes aren't washed and are all over the kitchen. In fact, I hate it so much that if I am preparing food I clean each dish, pot or utensil as I finish with it, while still preparing the food.

I am uncomfortable with an incomplete painting job. This discomfort makes me crazy until I finish it. There is a flaw, of course, in this logic. I then start another job, which is obviously not finished because I just started it. Duh! The whole season is back-to-back days of unfinished jobs, continual craziness, with only the periodic cookie of job conclusion.

I talk with a lot of contractors about a lot of things, one of which is bill collection. Some guys have trouble collecting. A lot of guys send bills through the mail. I can't stand the loose end of an unpaid bill. I need to get the check and cash it in order to put that job behind me, to cut the inner tie to that job, to make it history.

It isn't a matter of take the money and run. It's more like take the money and rest easy. I make no bones about warranty work, if it is needed. My customer service policy: anything a customer wants me to redo I do. It's that simple. I've learned that in business, whoever has the money has the power. And I have more faith in my honesty than anyone else's. I just need the final check to put my sense of closure on the job in order to rest in relaxation about it. Final payment slays the dragon of power over me and I am free to exercise generosity.

I have been taken advantage of in this business and have lost money. But I've learned from these mistakes and consider it an education. From this point of view, I paid for my education and I have never forgotten what I learned.

The second job I ever did I lost money. Just starting out, I worked alone. I remember working six long days for what I had estimated as an easy five day job, but the customer was not happy with the job and held back two hundred of the agreed upon four hundred dollars. The reason she gave was inadequate preparation.

I remember the conversation now, thirty years later:

>   She "You didn't sand the door!"
>   Me: "I DID sand the door. Perhaps you mean I didn't sand it
>   ENOUGH!"
>   She:" You didn't sand the door, you did a lousy job. Two
>   hundred dollars is a lot of money, that's all you
>   deserve!"
>   Me: "You can't do that. We agreed on four hundred!"
>   She: "You didn't sand, that's all you're going to get"
>   Me: "You arrogant jerk"
>   She: "Get out!"

Lesson: over!

Later that season I did a job for a couple in a very expensive neighborhood, who took exception to my trying to correct a minor problem. And not only did they take exception, but they took my money as well.

After completing the whole job, which by the way was done well, there appeared a little cedar bleeding in one (!) shingle in the rear of the house. The man of the house reacted as a man under attack and was indignant about the "defect" pawned off on him and HIS HOME by this so-called painter.

Naively, I thought I could just fix the mistake. I corrected it in the standard way of sealing the bleed with white pigmented shellac and then proceeded to repaint the individual renegade shingle. In my attempt at expressing good faith, I bought a whole gallon of new paint for this thimble-full job. Unfortunately, I failed to read the label because the paint store had given me a bucket of semi-gloss and not flat paint, both with identical looking labels. The result this time was a glaring error. Glaring indeed! He threw me out.

So I took him to small claims court knowing I was totally in the right. I had done the job. I had corrected the mistake but made another very small one. The fix for the second mistake would take a minute to fix, including coffee and cleanup. But he ordered me from the property warning me never to return, blocking me from completing the job and from my rightful pay. I eloquently told my story to the judge. The homeowner told another story.

According to this man, one shingle could not be repainted. He insisted the whole house needed to have been repainted in order for the paint "to be even", which he had already had done. "And here is the bill for the work", were his words accompanied by his display of a hand-written statement. This bill for service was a hand scribbled note on a piece of scrap paper, made out for some amount of money and submitted by some person named "Angel", who in my opinion certainly wasn't. How ridiculous!

But the joke was on me. The judge awarded in his favor and reduced his payment to me by the amount of Angel's hand written, scrap paper bill.

Lesson two: over!

In my second year of painting, I really took a hit! At that time I was already working with an employee or two. Business was good; I was getting referrals and found myself with an excellent job that had come through a decorator. This was the break I had struggled for and I looked at it as a very important account that I wished to cultivate. The job was a very large, high-end decorating job that I was ambitiously attempting with only one helper. I was seriously taxed, but the people didn't seem to care how long things took.

After a few days, though, my helper came to the untimely decision of answering his life's calling in some fashion other than painting for me. He quit just as this huge, important job was begun.

I tried out a couple of other guys, but after a few days of trying, it was clear I was better off alone for a while, so I went ahead solo. From time to time my girlfriend, later to become my wife, helped. Essentially I worked the job by myself. I spent about a month there.

Throughout the job the customers were agreeable and cooperative. She communicated about all of the details that usually arise in these situations. We caucused with the decorator. We coordinated with the remodeling contractor. Everything went along as a successful job in progress would. They approved the work I did as I did it, giving no impression other than approval. In time, this impression proved itself a house of cards as it came crashing down on me!

As I was finally finishing, at the end of about four weeks of work, their attitude turned decidedly critical. There were problems everywhere. They produced an extensive punch list to be corrected, but that was ok with me. I would take care of everything. It would take a few days but I was willing to put in the extra time to make things right. After all, this was a job from a decorator! I didn't understand that nothing I could do was ever going to make it right.

Upon finishing their list, like the Fantasia brooms, a new list appeared; and upon finishing that list, yet another. Like unwanted nose material on my finger, I couldn't shake off their demand for more work. They eventually began demanding correction of paint problems that were in areas not anywhere near the scope of the original job.

It finally dawned on me. Their attitude had gone from good to bad, and then, as I remained positive and compliant, they went from bad to worse. At that point I knew these people were out to get me!

I finally gave up at the three-week mark of endless punch lists, ready to punch someone myself. At that point I had put in eight weeks of work. They offered to buy me out of the deal for some small portion of my bill, which I accepted, amounting to the loss of more than a whole month's wages. At that time such a loss was devastating. I worked alone and had no other income. And these people had cheated me BY DESIGN! I couldn't have felt worse.

These people had out-flanked me in the war of business, and I hadn't even known there was a battle going on. At one point, he even took me aside to bestow the sage advice, "Don't take it so personally, Mike, its only business!" At that moment I was capable of hurting him badly.

I was so deeply wounded by the hateful, conniving cheat, I chose to avoid small claims court. I remembered my earlier experience there, so what was the point? I just wanted to avoid delaying the beginning of my healing, the forgetting all about these truly poisonous people. How naïve I was to not have known that such lousy people inhabit parts of my town!

But there were lessons to be learned from all of these experiences. And the losses received by each of them have come to be considered payment for knowledge. I truly paid for my education.

From the couple who house wasn't sanded I learned to always explicitly know a customer's expectations; better, if I have educated them carefully as to what to expect. Then work like crazy to ensure they believe they have received what they expected.

From the cedar bleed couple's house, I learned to never leave a mistake out for a customer to see. I follow a bit of Confucian wisdom: Never show a customer an unfinished job! (He called them fools, I call them customers, but in some cases one acts like the other.)

And the third couple taught me to manage my control of the job by controlling the money. People will treat you according to the respect they have for you. Money is the most powerful attention grabber for respect. Therefore, always charge a lot and always take large deposits and frequent progress payments.

NEVER leave a large amount of money owed to you. Always take a large deposit to begin, because this always gets their attention, softens them and makes them beholden to you from the get-go. And taking progress checks along the way maintains that respect. As long as you hold the money, they will not get mad at you. They can't, because in that situation YOU are THEIR customer. You owe them. It is the opposite of the standard seller-customer model.

Whoever has the money has the power. As long as you then display care and consideration when you hold the money, you establish an atmosphere of trust between you and them. If you are careful and smart, this carries over to the end of the job when they owe you again.

It is a way of turning the cards against the normal concept of the paying customer. It makes the seller the one who owes something to the customer. It requires the customer to be on his toes and polite, and not the other way around. I like this because I can then act graciously and generously, which in turn is always appreciated by the customer made to feel vulnerable by the reverse tactic. It establishes trust, which I seek, and that sets the tone for the entire transaction.

These are three big lessons I learned early on. I paid for them and they are mine. They are guiding principles for every customer I deal with.

RELATIONSHIP WITH CUSTOMERS

PART 2: RELATIONSHIP WITH CUSTOMERS

STARTING A BUSINESS

I never think about how I started in this business until I hear some bleeding-heart go on about the plight of the disadvantaged or the unjustly downsized crop of unemployed. Screw! Anyone can do what I've done if he or she wants to.

When I began I didn't even think of it as starting a business, I just needed some income. Being essentially honest, I intuitively understood I had to do something productive to earn the money and painting was how I would do it. At that time I was only several years out of graduate school and in the middle of defining myself as a cutting edge therapist for handicapped children. Painting was anticipated, and hoped, to be merely a very temporary fill-in solution.

I had had jobs, which carried position, authority and status. I knew exactly who I was and what I was about. But the rug got pulled out from under me when all of a sudden I no longer had a job or the opportunity for it. Who I was and what I was about I no longer was nor did. The door was slammed shut on me, effectively locking me out of the life I had taken so completely to be mine. I was literally cast adrift in a lost sea of confusion and doubt, unable to find "the right" employment. The shock of Life's removal of my chance to work with handicapped children was a vicious slap in the face that took years, no, decades to get over. At the time I was humiliated to not have this profession and then I was shamed to the core to have to go paint.

But I recognized my need. I had a family and as the cliché says I had to feed 'em. So I bucked up and I went door to door in the middle class suburb where I grew up. Day after day I knocked on doors to inquire about painting peoples' houses, pausing in shame almost to cry between buildings. After a while I developed strategies about how to do this that seemed to lead to more successful meetings with the home owners. But this was a very tough sell. Homeowners did not like strangers walking up to them to sell anything. Nonetheless, after a few days I finally got my first house to paint, and quickly got another. In this fashion I began my first job list and as one thing led to another I filled up an entire summer with houses to paint.

The point for me, as I remember these events, was that given the level of skill I had in painting, almost anyone with the desire could repeat what I had done. Anyone with the gumption could walk door to door and figure out through trial and error how to approach home owners. They could do it just like I did, and if they wanted it badly enough they would persevere until they had jobs. From this point of view, no one needs to be destitute from lack of employment. You don't have to paint: do carpentry, remodeling, roofing or plumbing. You could clean houses or just windows. You could cut lawns or plow snow. You could day-care children. There is an almost endless list of needed services just waiting for conscientious people to show up to do them.

And it isn't true that you need to be a master at it either. I was not a master painter, just merely good enough. I was a master of something else though: I was curious and asked questions. I asked endless product questions to the paint store counter people and I asked questions of technique and methods to other painters. I even acquired the reputation for it.

Maybe painting is easier than other trades in that there is no "right way" to paint. In a sense, any discussion of the right way is really no more than creative story telling. So, whomever you believe is the one with the best story.

There are different approaches to painting situations. There is a range of products whose specific choice of application is determined by certain definable criteria. There are technical factors for the various products. But there is no "right" choice, nor "right" method, since different products and even different manufacturers make the multiple choice quite multiple. All that matters is that the finished product not look wrong and that it should last a while.

The painter can pick any fruit of the product tree and adlib his application methods. He can describe it any old way he wants to. The product at the point of sale is words, the painter tells his product story. And what happens is that a painter's reliability and the level of confidence he inspires in his prospects and customers is more directly related to how he speaks about his work than to what he actually does.

This became apparent to me when prospects began to argue with me about the "right" way to do a job. This was displayed when sales prospects seemed to lose confidence in me to do the job after I had seemed to have won them over during the sales meeting. It dawned on me that they might be getting conflicting stories from other sources. Telling the most convincing story is the bottom-line key to getting jobs.

During the late 1970's and 1980's stained cedar siding became all the rage in new house construction. One of the sales pitches for it was that, unlike paint, it never peeled and was maintenance free. This is only a partial truth. Indeed it doesn't peel. Perhaps it could be said to be maintenance free, but only in the sense of being preparation free, because it does require re-coating. The requirement for preparation became evident, though, only as more and more of us professional painters dealt with the aging stained siding.

The underlying truth about cedar siding is confusingly multi-dimensional. If it is well sealed when it was stained originally, it should last four or five years without much deterioration of the cedar. However, all of the stain manufacturers of the time recommended staining new cedar a year after it was stained for the first time and only then going to a four or five year re-stain schedule; and it had better have been coated with the proper oil-based sealer!. If there is a "right way" at all to this, it is that in theory, wood can be expected to weather a given way when treated in a given manner. But when cedar isn't cedar at all, it may accurately be called siding, but it acts even differently than the above complicated expectation.

Sometimes home owners were misled or even lied to about the type or quality of wood used on the siding or any other house part, for that matter. If you add up all of the details of this story, you have the opportunity for any number of misleading, wrong or inaccurate facts about all of it. How could anyone possibly be expected to do anything "right" about this?

In theory, the painter should know what to do. But as you can see, house painting is far from theoretical perfection. Most of the time it is more fantasy since there is so much spin given to the sales pitch when, in truth, nobody REALLY knows much of anything true about what IT is, what is going on WITH it, and therefore what best in reality to do ABOUT it.

Early on I was staining a house in a nice well- to- do suburb. Everything proceeded more or less as expected. I had a couple of helpers and myself working on it and we were all done when a touch-up was required on the south side of the house. After finishing it we noticed a strange mark left by the ladder on the house. We put up another ladder to fix up the ladder mark from the first touch-up ladder and were left with another mark from this ladder as well. It quickly became clear that there was something wrong with the siding, the stain or the two together, rendering my finished job about as reliable as smoke in a windstorm. In fact, the homeowner caught wind of it and refused payment. I was stumped and went to the stain vendor for help. What happened next not only saved the day for me on this job, but it forged a twenty-five year relationship ongoing today with the vendor. It also taught me about mutual story telling.

First of all, I was a victim of the false storytelling regarding the longevity of stained cedar, since I also believed in the fiction about stained cedar being maintenance free. In other words, I didn't know the wood itself deteriorated and I certainly didn't know what to do about it. Secondly, the poor homeowner was the victim of some other false story telling. She had been told the siding on her house was cedar, when in truth it was some inferior, very soft and porous product, most likely balsa wood. Once covered with stain, someone must have thought, "Who would be the wiser?" But over time, its excessive deterioration revealed its non-cedar reality; but not before catching this poor painter unawares!

The upshot of it all was the homeowner had put off re-staining for an excessive amount of time. When I came to it, the outer surface of the siding had suffered deterioration, leaving it in a super dried-out, scaly condition that is the precursor of dry rot. In this condition, the wood developed a scale layer of "beat" wood fiber that resided on top of the solid wood that comprised the siding underneath the stain. Throw into this mix that it was balsa wood and not cedar, and we were left with a stain problem on steroids. This siding had weathered far more than it should have. Cedar would have performed in a similar way, but in that amount of time it would have shown far less deterioration.

The solution to this kind of stain failure is common knowledge now but at the time we didn't even know it was a problem. This siding needed to have been stripped prior to staining, a necessity we naively overlooked. Only since then has power washing become a standard practice in this type of job. Nonetheless, I had failed to perform this needed step and the stain that I had applied was adhered not to the siding but the scale. And like a slab snow avalanche, when the scale layer was scrubbed off with the ladder leaning on it, the newly applied stain came with it, effectively "polishing" the siding down to solid wood. This was the basis of the touch-up problem, which the stain vendor helped me correct.

With the vendor's help I learned how to recognize and take care of this kind of condition. But I gained something for more important. I learned how to speak about the stain problem in the same way as the stain vendor. In this I discovered a new level of professional distinction. When I spoke in the same way that homeowners heard him speak, it was verification or corroboration of my sales pitch and my professionalism, and it has won me more than one job.

In fact, saying the same thing as the paint store salesman has become one of my best sales strategies. I have extensively picked his brain on painting subjects from primer to paint, from chemistry to manufacturing, from application to tool selection. I want there to be not one gap, not one "holiday" or "skip" in the story I tell my prospects or customers and what they might hear from the store personnel. In fact, I take this so far as to develop a different sale's story to tell based on different paint stores, depending on where I anticipate the prospect going for advice. Since there is no single "right" way, each store and each salesman will tell a unique story. I want to coordinate my story with the "expert" authority my prospects will seek out.

After discussing a job at the time of sale, customers will often confess confusion regarding the differing opinions they have received from the different painters. I inform them that their most objective source of information is their local paint store. Funny how I wind up getting a lot of those jobs!

FAKE THIS AND YOU HAVE IT MADE

I don't know what I would do if my phone stopped ringing. I don't prospect, network, sell or do any of the things you're supposed to do to get business. I try to do a decent job, make my customers happy and be on intimate terms with my main supplier. I no longer approach anyone with solicitation. Nor do I want to do anything like that. Like my breath, requests for my painting services just happen.

If I were a controlling personality type, I would have to be out there making things happen. Instead I do nothing. The phone rings or it doesn't. It has always rung enough. It is as though I need not attend to acquisition of work, because something else will, or it will just take care of itself.

As the executive of my company, it is as though I have someone else, an assistant, albeit a fantasy person, who handles business acquisition. New-age, spiritual, esoteric people hold the notion of the existence of a more true, hidden, higher intelligence. In any case, it sure is helpful having a real assessment of what is in my power and what is not. In this case, I need not perform any direct action in order for this function to take place. The better I understand what is really up to me, the better will be my relationship with what does actually happen.

Sometimes business acquisition is like priming a pump. You put a little water in the system and pump like mad until water comes out. But, you might get water and you might not. I please customers and suppliers and my phone continues to ring. Sometimes it rings more than others. It just happens. Things just happen, or they don't, and it is up to each of us to make sense of it.

I recently read, though, that it was Groucho Marx who pegged the human race, and not the Dalai Lama, after all. Groucho instructed us: "The secret of life is honesty and fair dealings. If you can fake that you have it made. "

I wish I had a dollar for every time I have heard someone talk about doing the "right" job. Not only do I not have the dollar bills, but I also don't have the head-in-the-sand good sense of those who insist that there is a right and a wrong way to do things. That kind of thinking suggests that, for a painter at least, if you do less than the perfect job it says something about your character. It says that if you give less than everything you know how to do, then you are a cheater. In no other business is this measuring stick used.

When you go to the car dealer, if you order the car without leather seats or the navigation system, does the salesman throw them in because cars are better with them? If he permits you to buy the vehicle without these obviously better features, does that make him a snake oil salesman? No one would demean the character of the salesman for selling what the customer can afford. It ought to be no different with painting. But it isn't.

There is some unwritten rule that buying a paint job is like buying a piece of gum. One is the same as another; all you negotiate is the price. There is the underlying belief that even though one job costs $1000 and another costs $ 5000, they will be the same and function alike. The truth about paint jobs is as soon as you put the stuff on, it begins to fail. It's just a matter of time. But different approaches can put off the inevitable a little longer. Thus there is the objectively better paint job.

My job might last five to ten years. It could have points of failure in one. There really is very little control over some of the relevant factors, although the painter is always held accountable. If it peels in one, anyone would complain, "What a bum!" Isn't it true?

Consider the work of a dentist. He drills your tooth decay and fills the cavity, but the next week your tooth aches. So he does a root canal. The following week it hurts some more, so he reams it out again. Does all of the root canal work after tooth filling get performed for no cost because the filling is guaranteed? Is the guy a bum because the tooth filling didn't work? No, more was needed and he charged accordingly. But for some reason this logic does not apply for the lowly painter.

The painting industry as a whole suffers a systemic failure that finds its root cause in someone or another insisting upon their individual version of the "right" job that stands in opposition to their contractual partner holding a contrasting vision of that elusive perfection. Since we have already seen how there actually really isn't one, someone or another in the picture is seriously guilty of howling at the moon, in wild earnest. Remembering that the industry as a whole has largely been conducted by misfits, drifters and bums, it is easy to see how there is a general distrust and disbelief of the painter. Any conscientious painter-businessman needs to actively address these variables and this professional stigma, and for me it begins with the sales call.

There are sales techniques and methods. My approach is not to sell but to educate. I educate my prospect about every related feature of house painting. I take into account their expectations, and present them with options for achieving their goals along with the relative advantages and disadvantages of the optional choices. If they hire me it's because they believe I told them the truth. If they don't hire me it's because they don't believe me. Rule: there is no truth, there is no "right job"; it is just a matter of meeting someone's expectations.

Sales trainers teach salespeople to discover the expectations of their prospects. They teach how to interview the prospect to uncover his or her needs so that the sales offer can be customized to those needs. Most homeowners act as though they don't expect one paint job to be substantially different from another, so therefore there would be no individual expectations to cater to. In truth, though, they do have them, but much of the time they're more like hypnotic suggestions. They have expectations, but they are unconscious, they're unsubstantiated and they are most definitely undefined.

Take for example the word preparation. It has about as much specificity as the word weather. For a painter to say he will do preparation is about as meaningful as the guy in the double breasted suit on TV saying tomorrow we will have weather. But mention the word and the painting salesman passes that part of the exam.

21

To say you will prepare the house for painting can mean everything from a professionally done job of perfection to a pack of monkeys throwing paint scrapers around the yard. You'd be surprised how little of the one there is and how much of the other.

For many people if someone else uses a word, it is assumed they use it in the same way as they themself do, as with the word "preparation". And it is further assumed that if a painter uses the word and does mean it in the same way as they do, he will actually do what he says he will do,"I will, of course, do preparation...!" There is enough room in this for the painter-shyster to drive his truck through. Mention the few key words, and the average homeowner is convinced his house is going to get the same treatment as the White House.

There are two issues. First there is what the painter-salesman means by virtue of his using a particular word. The other issue is the likelihood of his actually doing what he says he will do. Already here there are two points of possible deception or strategic mis-representation, if you prefer.

I recently bid a job where the prospect informed me that my $6000 bid was being compared to a $2500 bid of similar specifications. I didn't believe for a second there was anything similar about the bids more than the other painter using a business logo he had stolen from me ten years earlier.

The prospect relayed that the other painter intended to follow all of the steps I had outlined, so he wanted me to explain why my job was so much more expensive. My approach to the explanation had two parts: one subjective, one hard fact. I began with the subjective persuasion of describing the actions of a crew of seasoned professionals under the constant stewardship of a conscientious, watchful eye and comparing that to the not so innocent antics of a pack of monkeys with paint bombs in their hands.

I portrayed the uneasy feeling of seeing the pack of monkeys drive up in their beat-up old van and parking the oil leaking relic on their freshly topped driveway. I conveyed the distrust inevitably to be felt as the monkeys were observed to step from their van with brushes, rags, tools, food wrappers and beer cans spilling from the opened door. I pointed out his inevitable head shaking to accompany his dumbfounded observation of the monkeys milling around the driveway and garage, spilling coffee from their Styrofoam finger toys. I pointed out the expected level of his pleasure in having not only the house being covered with new paint, but also the roof, the driveway, the shrubs, the windows. Only then did I resort to the objective facts.

My bid included a budget of $ 1000 for materials, including a line item of $150 for grinding discs alone. My labor estimate included a time estimate of one hundred hours of grinding and priming. These were the objective measures of my intentions. Simple comparison of my intentions to the other proposal yielded a simple conclusion: there was no way the other painter could deliver my specifications for the money he had bid. Trades contractors don't give away their time for $ 9 per hour. The prospect believed I would do what I said I would do; he gave me the job.

Belief is key, and how you deliver your message of intent is pivotal. Two summers ago I was having a bumper crop year of painting jobs. I had been on such a roll that I acted like I was invincible. I had inadvertently copped the wrong attitude one day during a sales call. I became overconfident and lost a job I really should have won.

The homeowner called me for the estimate. He was a busy small business owner, whose free time was as limited as mine. After a lot of phone tag and schedule incompatibilities, we finally found mutually available time for us to meet. His house was a perfect candidate for my approach. It was peeling like an onion and was in need of major paint removal. I estimated the job, outlined my proposal and waited expectantly for his approval. I don't remember polishing my fingernails, but I may have.

He didn't give approval. So I launched into a fall-back sales routine, which was to justify my price. I explained the whys, wherefores and how-comes which did nothing to budge his non-committed stoicism. In my discomfort, I began to squirm and reluctantly went into a self-praising routine, which seemed to only harden his unyielding position. Finally it dawned on me. The guy didn't trust me. He didn't believe me. Either he didn't understand the difference between what I meant by preparation or he didn't believe I would do it.

I think he didn't understand that my specifications for preparation are considerably more in-depth than almost everyone else's. The bottom line was he didn't believe me, which determined his decision. It was becoming clear to what degree that drives behavior and decision making. As proof, he didn't give me the job

During that time frame I estimated a job for a friend, which is always risky business. When I began to speak of preparation, she informed me that the competing bidder had also intended to prepare the house, raising for me the well-known red flag. She condescended that she knew full well what preparation was, at which point I gave up selling the job. Instead I politely accompanied her walking around and just discussing her house.

I didn't do the job, but a few months later I visited for a picnic. The house had been painted. As had curls of unattached paint that ought to have been removed. I was embarrassed to even notice. She had clearly received a poor imitation of a paint job, not worth it at any price. She thought preparation always meant one thing. Who knows if she even noticed what the other guy had done on her house.

But he had used the buzz word in his sales routine and she gave him the pass on it. Storytelling is key. What they believe, though, is up to them.

There are, of course, painters with integrity. There are those who will give a responsible job. Believe it or not, there are some who will throw in the leather seats and navigation system regardless of price. They don't do that for long, however, because they go broke doing it. They either leave the business or they change.

If you perform the job only according to the ultimate standard of perfection regardless of your price, you will much of the time be giving away services people aren't paying for. On the other hand, if you cater the job to the customer's expense expectations, you may not do enough. The contractor must achieve a satisfied customer, and his requirement is to arrive at a happy balance of their expectations, industry standards and profit. But you can never take into account all of the forces that work on a person. You will never take into account all of the pitiably weak ego factors that control some of your customers' moods.

I had painted an older woman's house several times when she referred me to her nephew. I waited for him to call me, which he did several months later. He had a cute little house in an established, highly educated upper-middle class suburb. It had some particular problems for which I proposed some innovative solutions. He was impressed with the labor intensiveness of my approach. And despite the padding of my estimated costs based on the labor time involved for those operations, he gave me the go ahead. It was a while before I got to the job, but it went smoothly enough. My crew put the necessary time into the labor intensive solutions and the homeowner was openly pleased with the result. He was so pleased he offered me the job of the complete redecorating of the interior of the place.

This was done in the fall. On this job, though, I dealt as much with the Mrs. as the Mr. The upshot was a successfully done job, which included a well done job of hanging wall paper in a very tricky room. Both of them were pleased. The money was forthcoming and everyone was everyone's best friend. That is until about six months later, when the couple had a dinner party and one of their not so gracious guests discovered what he considered to be imperfections in the joining of wall paper seams. The outraged mister called me on the spot. He apparently had to save face by making the complaint call in front of his goading friends. I agreed to see him, unable to even imagine the problem.

I arrived the following Monday to review their complaints which they delivered with a whole lot of bad attitude. The crux of the problem was the way the wall paper had been hung. Every inch of the painting was approved with their objections pinpointed on how the wall paper was hung. This was now a personal matter with me, since I had hung it.

Their friend had pointed out three areas where the pattern didn't match due to the seams not lining up. The couple insisted the paper was hung improperly and that anyone who would do the job that way was not entitled to keep the money. They wanted it back, six months hence!

Picture the room. It was a small dining room that had plaster walls. The two windows were casement type, but inset into the wall structure with curved arch plaster openings surrounding them, rendering the windows indented within the four or five inch curved arch plaster casings. There was an impressively sized mantle underneath, also of plaster. All of the plaster surroundings of the windows were obviously hand crafted, with the curves of the arches formed by more of a guess than engineering for consistency. In other words, the arches were not perfectly formed. Milled wood would have been perfectly formed, as would have been engineered steel or cast plaster. But hand-formed plaster could only be roughly curved, with less perfection of straightness, smoothness or arc than either milled or engineered pieces. In order to fit the wall paper into the casement windows, I had to custom trim it into these uneven places.

The paper had to be smoothed around and against the curve of the arch of the four sides of the window inset in the plaster wall. Where the paper on one side of a window's rounded corner met the opposite side-fold of paper each had to be trimmed before joining them together. This entailed sections of the pattern having to be removed prior to the remaining pieces being joined, thus resulting in a joined wall paper pattern that was comprised of two pieces of the paper that came from different, non-contiguous parts of the pattern. By necessity, the pattern COULD NOT match, and NEVER would. This was one of their complaints. The other had to do with the pattern not matching in one of the corners. No matter how I described it, they could not give up being screwed by me.

When you begin to hang wall paper, you have to decide where to begin. The decision is based on which location in the room is least noticeable, because where you begin is where you will finish. This matters because as you stretch the paper pattern around the room, strip by strip, ultimately you run out of wall. When you arrive at the end of wall space you have absolutely no control over the pattern that happens to show up when you hang and trim the last strip. Think about it! They didn't.

Invariably you must trim the last strip to fit the remaining last space and there will ALWAYS be a mismatch where the last strip meets the first. Typically this is done in an inconspicuous corner. How does an inconspicuous corner become conspicuous? I think the friend was just looking for trouble and found it in this corner. Our poor homeowner had a known identity problem of manipulable self- esteem. And the friend played him like a weak-ego fiddle. I was the unhappy audience.

The couple couldn't understand my explanation, or they just stonewalled in defiance. The wall corner was as good as it could be and the window cut-ins were solved with some very clever paper trimming. The so-called problems weren't a problem, but they refused to accept what their ego-violated logic demanded. They followed my explanations and seemed to understand the logic, but dug in their heels to insist on the only answer their friend had led them to accept. Return the money! When I look back on it, I think this may have been sport for the Mr.

Turns out, the Mr. is an attorney. He told me. First, he identified himself as an "attorney", which must be something more than just a lawyer. Right then I knew I was in trouble. And then he gloats that he can take me to court and even if he loses it will cost ME money to bring my attorney. Little did he know I would probably only bring a lawyer, but I didn't want to go that route.

We negotiated a buyout figure. He practically pumped his fists and almost high-fived his wife in his triumph, like he had just won the big one! But as he reached out to take the check from me, I scored some last minute points by pulling the check back a short distance, just out of his reach, but mostly in order to make a small point with him. Although I had no legal ground to stand on, I made him promise that the check would be the final restitution for him.

With the prize in sight, he agreed. In returning the check to within his grasp, his eyes practically rolled over in feeding frenzy delight, as I further made him promise to never call me again. Hearing him voice that promise was worth the money.

If it takes a village to raise a child, it might also take one to assess a paint or paperhanging job. I tried to actually do the right job, as opposed to talking about it. I had met the expectations of my customer, but he had failed miserably in his ability to meet the troublemaking expectations of his know- it- all, but know-nothing, friend. At any time, any customer can change their mind or be influenced. Mine had, and I just wanted to be done with the guy. The tagline of the story was, "I don't need his stinkin' four hundred dollars!" It was easier to pay him off than to keep looking over my shoulder in worry of his inevitable legal mugging.

BEING AN EXPERT

I am finally an expert. Surprisingly the status carries an unexpected definition. I have learned that to be an expert is not necessarily being able to do all things well. I don't have to know everything. But as a purveyor of a trade, I have to deliver everything in my craft to perfection. For me, being an expert means being comfortable with what I know but also knowing whom to ask when I don't.

By being able to either just do some procedure or to have adequate informational resources, I am able to be accountable to my projected image of painting professional. Although I do not at this point in my trade career need to ask many questions, I learned early the value of asking lots of them. As a matter of fact, I developed a reputation for being a very inquisitive paint buyer, and later a very knowledgeable painter.

At all points around the wheel of business I have to stand behind what I say, which translates into two rules for my help. The first is always to wear white pants, the accepted, conventional painter's uniform. But the important one is ALWAYS to do what you say you will do. I follow this rule to the letter. And since I wish to project an image of painting professional, I must know or at least be able to deliver everything included in my trade. This is a blessing as well as a curse. And in this duality is the need for knowing how to do everything or whom to ask when I don't.

Being an expert also has to do with never being wrong. I may not always know how to be right, hence the asking for outside expert advice. But I will never permit myself to be seen as wrong, or as not having done what I said would. Sometimes this means never going out on a limb alone; sometimes it means sending the customer.

At the point of sale, for instance, I don't sell, I educate. I try to educate the prospect's expectations. I avoid filling their heads with confusion in the usual sales manner of using a barrage of talk about all of the correct reasons for buying my superior service.

Sales like that are filled with a lot of bunk that will not happen, thereby creating false expectations. The typical sales pitch promises that which cannot be delivered. Far too many remodeling contracts end, or even proceed, with disappointment, animosity and non-payment. I avoid this.

I want customers to expect what WILL happen. Maybe we can call this honesty, but it isn't naiveté. It is a concerted strategy of complete and enlightened disclosure. Animosity and disappointment come from unmet expectations. Sales trainers promote the goal of uncovering a prospect's expectations, which I find useful, but not as important as educating them to have realistic ones. You need to find out what they want; you need to know what colors they want, to what standard they expect things to be done, as well as the specific details of the particular job. In this sense the professional trainers are right. But they need to be educated about what is possible, what is likely, what can be expected from the different alternative methods or materials, in short all of the technical aspects of the job.

I did a job for a lady who taught me about sharing expectations and acquiring information. She was an upper level manager in a high profile, locally-based, international corporation. She was high powered in her business role and she carried herself personally in that manner. I didn't respect her at first, though, because I thought she was a fool. She didn't know at all what she wanted. Or so I thought.

She kept asking my opinion for decisions the painter doesn't usually make. She would come out with statements like," I think I like this beige, with this white for the trim…although I could go to this mauve. What do you think?"

The complicated living room in her intricate old house needed some interpretation as to where to use the various trim colors. She would give me her ideas, but invariably follow them with,
"But what do you think?"

Every question I had for her, every decorating issue that arose, any either/or always led to her query, "But what do you think?"

She inevitably always made up her own mind. So it became comical to be constantly on the receiving end of her repeated the silly charade. I almost ceased giving her any respect or attention when she launched into this routine. It eventually became irritating to me. Only after many trials did I finally come to understand what she was doing.

She was unashamedly gathering information. She wasn't a flaky-airhead. She wanted another opinion, some outside information. She didn't want me to tell her what to do, but to assess her expectations. She was a world class manager who didn't need to know everything. She had her ideas, but she used an outside expert to bring them into action. I came to admire her style. And I have to admit the place looked pretty good when I finished it. So her style was effective.

I came to use this strategy in creative ways. I use it to gather information. I also use it to relieve myself of accountability.

I used to work for home- builders. I worked in high-end new houses that were very large, very complicated and full of expensive house parts. They were lucrative painting contracts and I enjoyed the high production environment required by those large jobs. But the potential for losing money was just over my shoulder the whole time. With as many as six men working at a time, hundreds of dollars of paint being opened each day, I was constantly sprinting to finish at least near the front in the daily profit race. The last thing I needed was costly mistakes.

Painting in and of itself is fairly straightforward. There isn't much that should go wrong, as long as you do things correctly and as long as you know what to expect. As often as I could, I employed a variation of, "But what do you think?" to avoid some potentially costly liability.

The large, expensive new homes I worked on were filled with large paintable spaces as well as other expensive house parts requiring other coating applications. Often, there was bare wood to be stained on trim and/or stair-systems.

Wood staining is more complicated than one might think. At first glance, it seems simple: you put on the stain, you wipe it off. This, however, describes the behavior, not the result. The result of this process varies according to a few factors which must be taken in to account to avoid preventable errors, because the corrections for which can be lengthy to do and expensive to pay for. Doing this work for my builders was a perfect case for employing a little "shared accountability" through a strategic use of "What do you think?"

There are different types of wood that are used for interior trim, with each having varying degrees of the relevant characteristics. Some varieties are so particular that they require special methods when staining, with varying procedures needed for them. In addition to these obvious complications, there are nuanced variations as well.

Any particular species of wood used for house parts will naturally show variations in color. In addition to the different grains of a piece of wood showing opposing colors, there will be light and dark spots in any individual piece and there will be lighter and darker examples of the variations of color from piece to piece. And when you add in the fact of varying degrees of porosity that determines how much stain color actually soaks into the wood, there is no way you can make these different pieces of wood all look the same without individually mixing stain for each individual color variation. And that just isn't going to happen anywhere in the reality of a painting sub-contractor's world. The problem arises, then, when someone wants his stained wood trim to all look exactly the same. I give them that option upfront of my doing it.

If you actually look at them, the individual pieces of a batch of the same wood look no more alike than a bunch of strangers waiting for a bus. But it is expected that these strangers should dress up and all look the same!

You hear such phrases as, "That's the beauty of the wood." which is an attempt to throw your mind off the fact that the different pieces of stained wood in the room don't look the same. But that's what you need to say *after* the work has been done, the spin you put on it after someone has already looked at the finished product and been disappointed. When you have to make this excuse to the one who is supposed to pay you for your work, more times than not you are going to lose the profit race.

To win, the builder must be educated BEFORE any of this work begins, to ensure his expectations are likely in line with what actually will happen. By giving him the heads-up first he has the option of paying four times as much for wood pieces stained with individually mixed custom colors or he can receive the standard stain job, resulting in a mixed bunch of strangers waiting for the bus. Either way is acceptable to me, making it clearly win-win: I do the normal job or work longer for much more money. In both the customer is satisfied, I get paid and receive a pat on the back. And I don't have to play catch up regarding the customer's unmet expectations.

KNOW YOURSELF, THEN KNOW YOUR CUSTOMER

In our culture, the idea of Karma might apply to account for some bad guy, like Hitler, getting his just desserts. But there is an aspect to Karma that has to do with the characteristics of our lives. This far-eastern religious principle accounts for the kinds of events, people and relationships that one attracts to one's self. In the field of doing business, I am convinced that there are right customers for a business person, and there are wrong ones. And who is right for one can be wrong for another, and vice versa. Getting to the right ones is the goal of marketing.

There are a number of ways to get business. One can advertise, network, cold call, subcontract and solicit in any number of ways. I have done them all and each is good for something, not necessarily for getting up-close with the best prospects. And each method can be done with more or less strategy and sophistication.

When I began, I went door to door in a middle class neighborhood merely asking the face at the door if they wanted their house painted. This was the simplest method done without much strategy or sophistication. When this crude method proved fruitless, I decided to think about it. Just a little analysis revealed the following: cold calling during the day would most likely find an empty house; cold calling during the dinner hour transforms the homeowner into the character of a dog who is separated from his food; and, cold calling at all takes people away from whatever it is they choose to be doing when they are recreating at home. None of these interruptions is a favorable circumstance for hitting them up for a paint job. Therefore, I decided to try only popping my question if they were outside their home and I could walk up to them. Doorbells were out, eye contact was in. I did begin to achieve some success, but it was limited. More bids were being given, a few jobs were secured, but the jobs were small or for a low price.

I put flyers in newspaper boxes and advertised in several small town newspapers with some success. But it was again measured only as an increase in the number of bids given. The jobs being won were more on the basis of low price than high quality. Thinking about it again I realized that the quality of my prospects was not good enough. I needed to attract interested parties who not only wanted their house painted, but wanted it done well and they wanted me, or at least someone like me, to do it.

It was around this time in my business life that I began to cultivate a relationship with paint stores. Most of my work was in a particular suburban area, so I used the main paint store there. I became known by them and eventually became friends with the staff and owners. I quickly began to receive referrals from them. This introduced me to a higher quality prospect that wanted a higher quality job and was leaning in my direction from the moment of their calling me. These sales calls allowed me to bid a higher quality paint job, with higher costs and to begin to raise my rates.

As this continued I began to build a clientele and eventually achieved the level of business establishment that I currently enjoy. Mine is now a business that is half referral.

Most businesses strive to achieve a fully referral business, but I count that as the weaker half of my work. The heart of my business is repeat customers. I have customers whose exteriors I have painted three or four times, and the interior over and over again as their whim has dictated. And in this pattern of repetition and referral I enjoy not only a high quality prospect who wants a very good job but they specifically want me to do it. And these repeat customers are old friends with whom I have a relationship. We are comfortable with each other and usually have much to catch up on. It is truly a lovely way to do business!

How is this accomplished? There certainly is no room for error in providing a quality product. In the process of doing so I work to achieve an unusually trusting relationship with my customers. This turns out to be my most important business practice. It is what makes them want me back again, even if I charge more than someone else. It is what makes them want me to do the job before I even give the price. It is the necessary antecedent for the service provider's golden request: "Just give me the price and tell me when you can do it."

It may be true that there are people who want a very good job, and are willing to pay accordingly for it. But it is also true that different types of personalities require a complementary personality style in their service provider. Not every painter can work for every customer, even if they are both on the same price-range page. The reason for compatibility is that each business person has their own customer. Mine are of a particular type and definitely not of other types. Some call this Karma, or life attraction.

I have been well established for quite a long time. A few years ago I received a referral from a friend of mine who is a very well established builder-remodeler. His customer needed his older house painted. It was a very large house and he wanted it done in the very best way possible. He turned to someone he trusted, and solicited my friend for painters. I was the one referred.

When I went for the estimate sales call, though, I was uncomfortable with the prospect. He made me uncomfortable. Something was amiss in how we related. I couldn't get a handle on the kind of person he thought he was talking to, what kind of person he thought he was, what rules of our budding relationship he was implying. All of this made me uneasy.

The job was so large, with so much money involved, and the fact of it being a new contract in the off season, made it an offer I couldn't refuse. He awarded me the job and freely supplied a large down payment on a job that would begin five or six months hence. Or so I thought.

When the time came for boots on the ground at his house he began to prove correct my uneasiness about him. He called me over to discuss the deal. I think the man had had too much time on his hands to think about it, because he had come up with some new ideas. They amounted to my having to perform more work for the originally agreed upon sum of money. It seems he thought he bought me for a price and could order anything to be done for that figure.

I held my ground because the extra work was substantial enough that performing it would have killed the sweetness of this job. He didn't seem to mind because he killed the job. But it wasn't a total loss, I assumed, because I was holding his deposit of several thousand dollars and believed I was legally justified in keeping it.

Push came to shove, and after the lawyers finished barking at each other I had to return three fourths of the deposit. The law works in funny ways. We made the deal, he broke it and I had to give up his good faith money. Good faith indeed! But at least my instincts were correct in smelling the bad fish from the get-go.

The interesting thing is that this man is a good and ongoing customer of my friend, who didn't understand my difficulty with him. What my friend failed to take into account is that each of us has his own customers. We cannot service someone else's. If the customer is one's own type, all can go well. If not, look out!

On the other hand, there are folks who from the moment we see each other, I know they are "my kind of people". I feel myself in a comfort zone where we seem to relate to each other on different levels. It is as though we are of the same tribe.

When you engage with someone of your own tribe there is no need to explain yourself. Of course there is the necessary sales pitch. But you don't have to explain yourself. You don't have to because your sales prospect already knows what kind of person you are. They get it, they're hip to you, they're on the same page, they speak your language, they understand you, they like the kind of person you are, and they trust you. There is a synergistic understanding, an unconscious-level agreement, with each other. The truth of this cannot be overstated!

When I approach someone I seem to greet them on at least two levels. There is the outer, ordinary level. This part of me says, "Hi. I am M.K. Nice to meet you", and all that. On the inside there is some very tricky and subtle, but very powerful, activity going on.

On the outside I am conducting the above conversation, behind that there is assessment: "Is this person safe?", "Is this person responsive to me?", "Does this person share my values?", "What does this person like and want?", "Is this my kind of people?". In short, I engage in evaluation of the prospect to determine what kind of person they are and the degree of our inner compatibility.

There are personality theories and psychological analyses, but my preference is to just look for a prospect's compatibility to me. The measure for this is "how" they are in respect to me, which appears to depend upon what they need from me in an inter-personal relationship. This might sound complicated, new-agey or esoteric, but I look at it as people being in a theater play. We are all in the play of our own lives. Plays can overlap or they can clash. Compatibility is when people who are playing their own roles get together with others who are playing their own roles, and everyone's roles are of a similar play.

With our behavior we interact with each other, but on the inside we inner-evaluate our degree of compatibility. Each of us plays the lead role of the play of our own life, and in our interactions with each other we evaluate the role and the play of others. When two people share the same or a similar play, they will feel comfortable with each other. Their roles will have a basis for relationship, as though they have already met, they understand each other, they're on they are same page, of the same tribe. All of this, of course, is unconscious level activity which cannot be directly observed. But looking at interactions in the context of individual plays sheds light on an area of business relationship that is ordinarily overlooked.

In one's play, there is the favorite lead character: one's self. Within the play, the lead character always acts to portray the characteristics of their role. At the same time, the lead role looks for the support characters that will portray the necessary counterpart to their lead. Some people have a lead character that is domineering and must decide everything. Some lead characters prefer shared decision making in an atmosphere of mutual trust. All of these characters naturally seek supporting characters who match up with their particular lead. For each lead character interviewing for a business contract, there would be right and wrong supporting roles: hence, the preferred customer or contractor!

I approach prospects with a sense of personal strength. Yet I am kind and am a gracious guest at their home. I am no one's inferior and I am everyone's peer. I don't care if you are CEO of a major international corporation, brain surgeon, or king of Siam. I will approach you with my full integrity. And if you happen to be a janitor at the local YMCA or floor-sweeper at Wal-Mart, I will treat you exactly the same as them.

I am smart and communicative. I am knowledgeable and considerate. I am not arrogant (just don't ask my wife), but I do not back down. Not everyone likes this in those whom they pay for services. Some prefer the character of servant. I don't play that role well. For those who prefer that, I am not their painter. And that is why my builder friend's customer was not right for me. He wanted a servant, not one of my available character parts. Had I been able to play that part, I am sure the job would have proceeded well. It would have come out all right and I would have made my money. I just can't play a good servant.

By not being able to play the prospect's preferred servant-character part, and he not being able to play the corresponding mutual-partner role I prefer, we were uncomfortable with each other: there was a clash of our individual plays!. He required someone he could rule, but I am sure, still pay at the end. I required someone with whom I could discuss and work things out with together. It was an unavoidable conflict. We all are in the play of our own life, and we seek out those who supply the corresponding characters for our main character, ourselves. When people meet, they are comfortable with those whose play provides a character that corresponds to their own play. When the person you meet puts out a character from a contrasting play you don't get along. Not only can you not fish out of two streams but you also cannot appear in two plays at the same time.

Trust is an interesting issue and vital to contracting services. Trust cannot be bought. But it can be earned or just be there. If it looks like a duck and quacks, it is a duck. And if you, as sales representative for your own service, look like whom it is they already believe are trustworthy, then you are. And when this happens without subterfuge, in other words, when it happens genuinely, it is the proverbial fit made in heaven.

When you are with customers like this it is like putting your hand in an old glove. You still have to do the task at hand, but at least it feels good to be there. You feel the naturalness of the fit. With that deeper level of relationship, the service provider strives to maintain a level of trust as opposed to building one. When you don't begin from behind an eight ball it's a lot easier. I look for this when I meet a new prospect and walk away easily when it is not there. I like my ducks to quack!

WHAT GOES AROUND COMES AROUND

There is a wonderful relaxation that accompanies honesty. When one is relaxed there is an enhanced sense of freedom in action as well as decision making. And this freedom stems from a deeper sense of openness in one's self that not only comes from honesty but produces it. This stuff is fairy dust! Open honesty can arise within a person, or it can jump from one to the next. When a sales job becomes a session of this spontaneous genuine-ness, everyone is put at ease. This is what I seek in myself. My selling strategy is to accomplish this.

As I have said, my sales approach is one devoid of sales. Instead I educate. But if information is education for the prospect's intellect, a calm demeanor is a message to their emotions. On the one hand I want the job, but not at any cost. I want the job but not if it isn't a good fit between them and me. Sometimes our personalities just clash. Other times there is a requirement for me to find an inner attitude that not only puts them at ease, but me as well. My words speak to their minds, but "how" I am can establish a different, deeper kind of connection.

I find there is a direct relationship between my degree of relaxation at the point of sale and the prospect's feeling relaxed. Since most ordinary sales pitches tend to be high pressured events of competing, dominating storytelling, my relaxed but highly informed approach can actually reach some people in desirable ways. What it touches in them is their emotions. My relaxed presence speaks to their emotions to indicate that I am honest and trustworthy. When this happens the prospect also proceeds through an inner loosening that allows them to feel my non-attacking, non-competing, non-dominating, collaborative sales presentation. At that point I have essentially won them over, and it is only a matter of agreeing on the details.

I have a customer whose house I have only painted once, so far. It was about ten years ago, but I see him often. We cross paths from time to time around the small village where he lives and I work, but he has never mentioned painting his house again. I would never force the issue by asking him about it, choosing instead to avoid putting anyone on the spot. Finally, he called to ask for an estimate.

As we walked around the house I remembered the job when I did it the first time. I remembered some of the particular details and I especially recalled the problems we had had there.

His house suffered from "unsealed paint syndrome", a painter's kind of UPS. After all of my usual very extensive preparation, we painted the place. This is usually the "cake" part of the job but in this case it was a frustration. As the finish paint began to dry, in many places there developed bubbles. But these were not simple air or moisture bubbles in the fresh paint. These were bubbles that occurred in the base layer of paint. This only happens for one reason.

When paint is put on bare wood, it is supposed to be a primer as well as a sealer. Primer paint is the first coat of paint, whose function is to stick to the wood. Primer paint is formulated with the specific ability to bond to whatever it dries on. Primers are designed for different materials, so you must choose the appropriate one for whatever it is you are painting.

The other function of the primer is to seal the material it is put on. In addition to sticking to what it is put on, this first layer of paint must "close the door" of the material. Nothing must be able to either come out of the painted surface or into it from the surface. It must be sealed.

Any piece of wood will have resins or other vapors that must be "locked in" to the wood so they won't seep out and stain the finish paint. In addition to keeping those in, the sealer must also keep out any foreign liquids or vapors that might settle on the surface that might be absorbed into it. Technically, the primer-sealer fills the pores of the wood in such a way as to eliminate any transfer of liquids or vapors, either into or out of the painted material.

My customer's house had not been sealed properly by the original painter. When I painted it with even the finest water based house paint, the water in this coating penetrated the existing paint layer. It penetrated right on through the top coat and down through the first, which may have been a primer, because it was against the wood. But this primer failed to prove it a sealer, because the water of the fresh paint penetrated it and wet the wood. When the resulting vapor evaporated from the wood trying to dry itself this caused the entire multi-layered coating of paint to bubble. It was a mess. I had to correct it. I did. The customer appreciated it.

As we toured the house this time, for the second painting, we recalled that earlier battle and how it had been resolved. I was able to completely convey the thoroughness of my approach, because he had already experienced it. In a sense, this estimate tour was a reminder to both of us what I had done. And in that mutual remembrance we were both impressed.

By feeling impressed by what I HAD DONE, I was able to speak about it in a very real way, not one of arrogant pride but a simply honest professional pride. I spoke about it as one who genuinely appreciates the very thing he is trying to communicate about. In other words, I was brought to an inner feeling of genuine appreciation for the product I wanted to sell. This genuineness was felt by him as well.

I chose to remember what I had done and to appreciate it. This remembering in the moment is an action I make on purpose and by design. I see it as a piece of active, inner self-awareness, awareness of myself by myself. I open myself to experiencing the truth and then allow myself to feel the strength of that. It is a kind of Zen moment, and it brings me to a "real" feeling of appreciation for my approach and what I do. It is far better to convey what you really feel. On purpose I generate this, because it may not just happen on its own.

At that point, we sat down to talk it over. As we did I felt both of us relax. I relaxed because I had nothing to hide or pretend. I was merely trying to convey what I will be able to do for the nice man's house. He became relaxed, I believe, because he was not being assaulted to accept another man's will. There was no battle of the wills, nor any battle at all for who needed to be right, or whom wrong. This kind of relaxed, non-competitive, collaborative conversation is a proposal for partnership. Prospects appreciate it. My customers love it!

Elsewhere I have spoken about my customer base and that it is only a half referral business. This is the weaker half of it, with my preferred customer being the repeat ones. These homeowners have already discovered my basic honest approach and they trust me. I have already proved myself to be trustworthy and they haven't the stomach or the need to look for someone else to supply the service. But I have mishandled this, too.

I had a customer whose house I had painted quite a long time ago. As I recall it had some particular paint problems stemming from the prior painter having used floor paint on the entire exterior, thereby leaving an overly hard, brittle very thick paint layer that required a lot of extra effort to be made right, which I willingly did. When they moved to another house they had me paint it.

I did the exterior and, room by room, most of the interior. Clearly I was their painter. When they wanted something painted they even gave me the contractor's golden egg: "How much will it cost and when can you do it?" At some point they stopped using me. Unfortunately I know when.

During a busy period I was there with a few helpers painting some rooms. This was a one hundred and fifty year old house whose bedrooms most likely had not been painted in a third of that time. The plaster was bad, too, requiring extensive work. The old, wooden windows were very peeled and chipped, needing a lot of hours of attention to correct before putting on paint. I recall three guys spending two days fixing up the windows and trim, while I stepped in to make the fine wall patching. All proceeded well and correctly up to the point of putting on the paint.

In those days trim paint was always oil based. The transition to water based paint had only proceeded as far as wall paint, with oil based paint still offering the finest finish for brushed trim. A nice finish it had, but it was also a magnet for airborne dust. In this case it was also put on over windows whose wooden sash bars had become wet from frost condensation. The combination of water and dust gave the paint something other than a nice finish. You might say that all of the preparation work my guys had done was two steps forward that was followed by two steps backward from the moisture and dust. What they had done was un-done, and it happened when and after they painted.

Three men had spent a whole day painting these pieces in addition to the two days of preparation. To redo it would have been expensive, involving a couple of days of work for the three. I felt I was responsible for the problem and that the fix was mine. It would be up to me to cover the expense of the extra time to correct the problem and I just didn't want to. My reasoning was that since these were spare, out of the way, bedrooms, I could leave these less than perfect windows in their sorry and unjustifiable condition. They paid me but I never heard from them again.

Violation of trust is an assault on the emotions. Once it has occurred, the deal is done. If paper covers rock, rock breaks scissors and scissors cut paper, then violation breaks trust and that is not made right by logic. It was simple oversight amplified by a bad decision, and it cost me a very good customer. More importantly, it proved me untrustworthy to them. That cannot be made right again. Nothing I can do will restore their trust in me. I don't deserve it for what I did.

THE GATEWAY

It's nice when the phone rings. Most of my business now comes to me from the handheld talker and I sometimes forget the thing is inanimate. I act as though IT is supposed to DO something. Obviously, the phone is way down the chain of command and somehow my job is really to get to who is holding the can on the opposite end of the string.

When I started painting I didn't use the telephone. I didn't use much strategy at all. As described earlier, my default sales tactic was to present my unknown face at someone's door, which was an approach that failed to promote desirable contracts. The deals people would make with an unknown face tended to be ones a familiar face wouldn't accept. If beggars cannot be choosers, then door to door sales people have to take what they can get. This form of business acquisition is no more than begging. The jobs I got in this fashion were crumbs, feeling an awful lot like something being dropped into my upside-down and open hat.

I felt like a beggar. How nice it would be, I thought to myself, if homeowners knew me when I arrived at their door, or if they even WANTED or expected me to be there. How nice if someone called ME! These innocent daydreams weren't naïve pipe dreams at all, but the stuff of real business. And it was in those directions I decided to focus.

I didn't waste any time, I began to inquire about advertising. I started with the city-area newspaper. WOW! It was expensive. A full-page ad was totally unaffordable, as was a half, quarter or any other fraction of a page. Luckily there was the want ad section, but what was the point in putting a few words in about calling me when there were twenty or thirty other identical little ads to call other painters. With all of those ads looming basically the same, picking one or another was on the level of reaching in to a grab bag. I understood I needed to distinguish myself in those ads. And I needed to find an affordable venue.

I was trying to work in the neighborhoods I knew, which happened to be in more affluent parts of town. There were two small, neighborhood-town newspapers that serviced these areas whose advertising rates were a whole lot cheaper than the city paper. But I still couldn't afford any portion of a page advertisement. I reluctantly settled on a simple, cheap want ad.

I remember at first using combinations of capital and small letters of varying sizes thinking I was distinguishing my ads in that way. Later I used a copy of my business logo that was designed to stand out in a crowd. Perhaps it did stand out some, but it was still a grab bag of a long list of painters looking to take peoples' money.

Work did come from this advertising. But all that was different from door to door begging was that they had read my name in the paper. My face was still unknown as was I, the person. Business acquired in this fashion is always low end, cheap price bidding for a bare-bones job. The bottom feeding shoppers attracted to these ads are basically just fishing for paint jobs offered for the smallest number. These paint jobs need to be of minimum labor in order for a painter to work for the price shoppers would pay. These jobs were nothing more than putting lipstick on a pig.

During this first stage of my business life, advertising was my main source of jobs. I had heard other painters brag about how once they get a job on a street they then canvass the neighbors for more. Since I already knew about "begging for jobs" I had to branch out in other ways. I thought about it. If you want to catch fish, you go to the stream. If you want to pick flowers you go to the garden. If you want anything, you have to go to where they hang out. Where do homeowners in need of paint jobs hang out? Hello paint stores!

In my immediate neighborhood there was only one major paint store where I bought my paint. It was there that I not only went for help finding sales prospects, but I began to use the store salesmen in my unique way of asking a lot of questions. At first, I just wanted to bolster my sales approach to prospects with knowledge. The unexpected side effect was I also became familiar to the paint store salesmen and quickly became on first name basis with them. These were whom homeowners talked with when they came to the store. These men became my first gateway to job prospects.

I was definitely the new guy on the block. Unlike these days, then there were a lot of house painters and this store was busy with them. If there was a list of preferred painters, I would have been at the bottom of it. I did get some referrals but not enough to eliminate advertising. I wondered about other gateways.

Where else would homeowners in need of a paint job hang out? Who else is close to that crowd? In my travels I began to meet decorators. Some I met at the store and through networking conversations got onto their short list. Some I met through homeowners. But they are a fickle lot whose expectations clearly were that they would always feed first and anyone else can have leftovers.

My relationships with all of the decorators I dealt with fizzled out after some time. Some relationships lasted only a job or two, some a few years. I think they could be an excellent gateway for the right painter with the right personality for the particular decorator. I never achieved the degree of personality match-up required for a long term relationship. I think I was always much too independent. In other words, I found it difficult allowing her to feed while I played the role of servant. I'm sure, at this point in my maturity, that I could do my part in that dance a bit more elegantly. Definitely, I was burdened with a personality flaw that interfered with those business relationships. Had I been savvier, or at least more mature, those contacts should have continued to be productive.

I also sought out builders and contractors. But if decorators were prima donnas, these guys were sharks. They would always get you for a low price and then squeeze you for free extra work. By delaying payment, these sharks would always owe you money and they would make that payment contingent upon your fulfilling a little piece of "good will" for them. They were masters of this kind of extortion and to get the work I had to take care of their needs. With all of these gateways, a young, inexperienced person trying to become a successful business person will always be outfoxed and taken advantage of by the more experienced contractor or decorator.

In my second year I met a big time commercial builder-contractor at the counter at the paint store. He was building his own new house and was looking for a residential painter. He had his regular commercial painters, but he knew their work to be hack. They were GE, *good enough*, for commercial application but not nearly nice enough for someone's home, let alone his own. We talked, we met at the house, I got the job. I didn't get quite as much as I wanted for the job, but he dangled the possibility of a long term relationship in front of me as part of the compensation package.

The job came out pretty good. There was nothing to complain about, which is basically what a good paint job is. But no additional work ever came from it. I learned that promising more work is the contractor's euphemism for price reduction. When the buyer offers more work in the future it is because he intends to reduce the price for the current one. And there usually never is a next one. This job came out fine but I never heard from him again. He hooked me for less than my preferred price by offering a false promise. How naïve of me! I was fooled the once, but not twice by that ruse.

I continued in this way until I bought a home closer to another store and closer to the most affluent suburbs of our area. As I started with this new store and in the new area, I already knew about using gateways. It turns out the store owner understood this as well, because he spread the referrals around to a lot of grateful painters hanging around his store. As my use of his store continued, so did the increase in frequency of referrals from him. It became clear that as a gateway to jobs, this store, this paint man, was a fountain of work. Like standing outside the stadium turn-style after a busy game, homeowners flowed either in person or by referral and I began to receive more and more work from him.

One of the consequences of this way of getting business is that by inference, I represent his store. In addition to my work not only determining my relationship with the customer, it also reflects back on the store. In order for me to get paid I had to do a good job. But to get more referrals, I needed to be excellent. One referral is always appreciated; it gets me a job for today. But taking care of tomorrow, and the days after that, is more important. Therefore I had to become excellent. More than that, I became uniquely excellent in developing a painting product that went far beyond what anyone else did. I learned how to take care of my customer in uniquely caring ways. All in all, I gave the paint store no reason to NOT refer me and every reason TO refer me. Twenty five years later I enjoy the status as top dog on the referral list of this paint store.

PEOPLE ARE CRAZY, DON'T HAVE EXPECTATIONS

People are crazy, whether it's underprivileged and dysfunctional trades' employees or their bosses, or the people that hire them. Homeowners will have the cockamamie-est ideas about everything. Take your pick: at any time a home owner will know better than a thirty year pro how to paint a house, what to use, in what conditions or what proper technique is. I had someone once "catch me" rolling paint on his house. His idea was that only brushing is legitimate. I had a homeowner size me up once, literally. She informed me my ankles were too small for this kind of work. There is no telling what controlling ideas roll around in someone's head until judgments start spilling out in the form of their words or actions.

One fine summer day I had a nice job going that was comprised of the exterior staining and painting as well as the painting of a large portion of the interior. This was an excellent opportunity for me to strategically use my help in the two areas, focusing the experienced helpers on the technical and complicated tasks, while using the less skilled guys for the simpler, no-brainer work. I had forged the deal with the gentleman of the house and had not even met the Mrs. until I showed up to work the first day.

She was pleasant enough as my crew and I unpacked and had at both sides of the job at once. I had a couple of the less experienced guys begin some preparation work outside, while I worked inside with a couple of guys who knew which end of the paint brush to dip in the bucket. We finished the day having made almost a day's progress, making it close enough to a day's quota for me to call it a day's work. She thanked me for our efforts and our progress and sent me off thinking I should be feeling ok about myself. That night I received a telephone call from the mister that blew that theory out of the water.

It seems that when his darling wife complimented me on the day's work, this wasn't a fair representation of how she actually felt. In fact, it didn't at all say how she felt. Little did I know, she must have been speaking in opposites! Either that or she had omitted her evening dose of Prozac. She now had nothing positive to say about the day's work. The exterior preparation was inadequate, there were problems on the inside work as well. In this crisis of loss of trust, I immediately went to them to talk it over. Once there, the fun really began as she tried to level me with blame and criticism and he tried to override the damage of her foul demeanor to keep me on the job. As she continued to hammer me with below the belt punches, he sat by her side until he couldn't take it any longer.

He finally sent her from the room so that a legitimate effort could be made to salvage a solution. With her out of the room, hammering me was unneeded as he apologized for his wife's foulness and begged me to continue. Considering the Mrs.'s attitude, my terms for continuing were simple and clear: I required full payment for what I had already completed and wanted regular progress checks along the way, and SHE needed to stay out of my way. He agreed, wrote me a check and called her in to inform her of the deal. She didn't say a word but I swear I saw fire in her eyes and smoke coming out her nostrils. She was self-controlled enough to hold it in as I left for the evening. She was spitting venom in the morning.

As I drove up to the house in the morning I saw her on patrol, pacing as she awaited me, her enemy. She wasted no time in drawing the battle line, pronouncing that SHE, not her husband, was conducting this deal. That SHE would decide when or IF I would be paid, that she was calling the bank to stop payment on the check and only when I jumped through her hoops would she even consider what my payment would be. I was shell shocked, sizing up the path she had set in front of me!

I took the guys close around me as if to give out job assignments, but really to whisper to them to only go through the motions of setting up, not to dip brush into paint or make any mess requiring clean up. I wanted them to buy me time to cash the check before I pulled out of the job. Once they were engaged, I confronted the lady. I informed her that stopping payment on the check at that point constituted fraud, that it was an arrest-able offense. I declared my intention of cashing the check immediately while the job was being continued, and that if she stopped payment I would return with a State Trooper who would haul her away on the spot for this crime. I had no idea if she took the warning bait as I drove off.

I sat on the edge of my truck seat as I made my way to her bank and then held my breath until the teller handed over the several hundred dollars, the victory flag in this game. I returned to the job, packed up the gear and the guys and pulled out over her objection and continued ugliness.

Being Friday, I paid the guys for the week, but also bought a few cases of beer and proceeded to get drunk with them to wash this nasty, fairy-tale witch-lady out of our minds.

That night the gentleman called to beg me to continue. At first I declined, but then gave conditions for finishing: complete payment in advance and *wifey* never home. Still feeling the afternoon beers, I changed the conditions to: DOUBLE payment, I would refund as much as I chose and I didn't care if she was home. He knew he was checkmated, apologized for her behavior and said goodbye as he was mumbling something about, "…the last time she will…", "…having had it…" and " …leaving her for good…".

You never know where you will find trouble. Sometimes it comes from the employees, sometimes from the homeowners and sometimes it just finds you. At another time we had just finished a hard job in the humid heat of the height of summer. It was so hot and the sun so scorching, it seemed that no matter where you walked around that house, it was in the direct sun. Our bodies cooked, our foreheads toasted as we ground down the old peeling paint and labored to apply the fresh stuff. It was a blisteringly hot week of grinding, squinting and choking. It was parched, hard physical work that theoretically is supposed to be an aesthetic touch of decorating art.

Finishing it, I wanted to do something nice for the guys, meaning I wanted to give them something extra. I bought a few cases of beer, went to the beach with them to unwind, cool off and drink up.

We went to a nice free beach on Lake Ontario, popular with beach goers all summer long. It was a Friday afternoon, there were a lot of people but we found a spot where we could do our thing. We drank the beer as if someone would come take it away. After a while a bottle of something or another appeared. The party was on!

Guys were playing hacky-sack. Guys were swimming. I was having a seemingly mature conversation with one of them. As one of the crew was playing hacky-sack, the group of guys next to us began playing Frisbee. There was a big, nasty looking guy playing with a small wannabe-nasty-looking guy. The two of them tossed the fris back and forth but were getting too close to our guy Chad who was still knocking around his hacky-sack. These two nasty looking guys circled around until Chad was between them. It was at this point that it became clear that something sneaky was happening. Aaron, my conversation mate looked on shaking his head, whispering to me, "They had better not piss off Chad!"

They tossed that Frisbee back and forth now with purpose. As the inevitable almost finally happened, I could feel Aaron go rigid as we both watched the Frisbee sail just over Chad's head. In our relief, Chad picked it up and calmly tossed it back to one of them as we expected the worse which did not have a chance to go down. It didn't because a more compelling one was developing out in the water.

A few of our guys and a few of theirs were playing on a log that happened along. Boys being boys, competition grew out of who might be the only one at a time to stand on top of it. King of the log proceeded until the ordinary, harmless means of play became old hat. Escalation proceeded until one of theirs punched one of ours. Bloody-nosed, Mark called the water puncher to dry land to settle it, I'm sure, once and for all!

They fought. Well, if this fight were a dance it would be one of those where someone prances around with a figurine for a partner, with the person dancing while carrying the other along for the ride. Mark was along for the ride. We tried to stop it. But with Mark screaming, "… but he's an asshole!", and being so drunk, he was down on his back with the other guy pummeling his head almost immediately. After watching a few drunken swings, Aaron declared the fight over, pulled off the other guy declaring him the winner. But the hornets' nest had been poked.

Before anyone had another thought, the big nasty guy picked a fight with Bobby, a small, wiry guy from our side. The big guy was big, but dumb. He was probably drunk, and therefore dumb and drunk. When Bobby, in his tough macho street style, signaled his willingness to throw down with the big oaf, the big guy turns his back to Bobby, declaring his intention to, "put some music on first..." (No lie, he said this). This back turning was so inviting to Bobby he began right away wind-mill-punching the big dumb guy into a sleeping giant imitation. And then all hell broke out. There was tension everywhere: pushing, shoving, posturing, arm pit scratching and lots and lots of other guys showing up. Our opponents must have had protection treaties with neighboring beach toughs, because we were suddenly surrounded by a lot of nasty looking guys, all facing our way.

It was when one of them came up to me with hopeful intentions that I thought things would improve. It was when he started out with, "Hey, I'm older, you're older..." that I breathed easier in anticipation that he would say something about us talking sense into those young hot heads. But the dream ended when he finished his statement with something about our mutually advanced age making us equal fighting partners.

At this, one of my guys stepped in to keep us off each other. Anything goes in a street fight, but as in chess the king is off limits. My guy swept me out of there, up the hill to our trucks. We were followed by this swarm of nasty guys but managed to get out of there without being chased. It may have been the few bottles of beer we tossed on the grass or maybe it was the bikinis and halter tops that came for the show, but something kept those nasty guys where they stood. We were lucky to get out of there. People are crazy and there is no telling what crazy ideas roll around in their heads.

But crazy isn't limited to street toughs or anger-mismanaged homeowners. Maybe it's universal. Crazy appears all over, and you can expect it in the most unexpected places.

I painted a house for a couple who had hired a decorator to decide the colors. Why people do this is beyond me, but then again I don't understand why most people do most things they do. But they needed someone to tell them what colors they would like.

Skipping to the bottom line, the house wound up with three of the most garish colors I have ever seen, let alone together. Maybe there had been a contest for awful colors, these three were on the top of the top ten list and, in indecision, the decorator just threw all three of them on the house. Or maybe it was some cruel joke.

Consider this: a lime green body, puke brown beige trim and some nondescript mauve-orange-peach for shutters and doors. The house burned to the ground a year or two later. I have always suspected the neighbors.

This decorator was a unique piece of work. She was a bit older, maybe seventy. She was always dressed like a magazine fashion statement, but drove up in an old ratty jalopy. If she were caviar, she served herself up on an old baseball mitt. Maybe she didn't think anyone noticed her conveyance. Maybe she didn't realize her choice of chariots drained the belief out of her little act of elegance. Her behavior didn't add much either.

She always wore large sunglasses. Every time she showed up, she had on the darkest lenses you have ever seen anyone wear. There is nothing unusual about important people wearing shades, but she insisted on looking through them when examining colors.

Usually when I start a job, colors have already been selected. The last thing I want to do is hold up a job in progress, I mean guys on the payroll, while the home owner taps her chin and cutely declares she just can't decide. In this case it was the hired hand whose finger tapped her chin, said I just don't know, all the while hiding behind her shades.

Every sample I showed was followed by the chin stroke and upward gesture of the hands. Finally I sent the decorator to the paint store to avoid my running back and forth.

She entered in sartorial flamboyance, complete with the stylish oversized shades. She explained to the paint man behind the counter her vision for the perfect color, he complied with a sample. She examined, then instructed darker, bluer, whiter, redder, as he adjusted and adjusted. With each new rendition she examined, but never did she remove the dark glasses.

What a joke it was, to see her examine the color and declare it too dark. You could have welded in those glasses! The entire world would be dark through them, making it impossible to see anything, let alone color detail. But she laughed derisively at the final sample, wrote it off as too dark. She disapprovingly passed judgment on the paint man's color work, "You went too far with it. You'll have to start over." She is lucky he didn't throw it all over her. But she probably wouldn't have noticed because she wouldn't have seen it through those lenses.

Instead, he left her alone with the color sample while he and I went to the back room "to check something". After we had left the room, she looked around quickly before she lifted the glasses, practically touched her nose to the sample as she gandered at the color, and moved it back and forth and around her face in the vicinity of her eyes. It was more like a tactile examination than visual. We watched from the back and when she finished we reappeared. She never let on, but her acceptance of the color came at that point.

It was some time later that the paint man informed me what he had seen that I had not. At some point during her viewing process, she lowered her glasses quickly again but in view of my friend behind the counter. What he saw was the icing on the cake. Her one eye was crooked, pointing almost directly to the side. She covered it to hide that fact. Imagine what people would think if she held up a color sample to the side of her face and declared, " yup!. I like it". She couldn't do that. So instead she faked it. And when she thought no one was looking, she looked at it in earnest. But we caught her. I never did feel proud of myself for that. You never know where crazy will show up; sometimes it is in you.

PRICING A JOB OF INTEGRITY

Pricing a paint job is funny business. It's not like pricing a car, for instance, or a refrigerator, or a shirt. There are list prices for those products that are all established by the manufacturer. Maybe the final cost is negotiable, but the prices are fixed. There is no "price" for painting. Painting isn't an item, it isn't factory manufactured with each individual paint job identical to all of the others.

Early on I had asked a seasoned pro, an industry insider, how to price jobs. I was entering the subcontract world of custom new homes and I wanted to know how other painters did it so I could compete effectively. The answer wasn't what I wanted to hear, but what I needed to know. My friend told me to get as much as I can for the job. This wasn't the formula I wanted, but it was the spur I needed to figure it out for myself.

Subcontracting prices in commercial work is highly competitive; residential painting is much less so. Since I am the manufacturer, I can price the job as I wish, with the upper limit of pricing being what the market will bear. The necessity is to price my work at a low enough level that produces enough work to keep the crew always busy, but at high enough price to be interesting and motivating for me. This typically becomes a subjective game of how much is not too much!

Comparative pricing is the only measure most homeowners have for price evaluation. Therefore, there is no true industry standard, only industry sampling. The homeowner's concept of industry standard ends up being the comparison of the several estimates he or she collects for a given job. Industry standard is reduced to an unknown variable that fluctuates with the painters interviewed.

At any given moment, the standard encompasses a range of hourly rates that vary from $ 20 per hour to $50. Industry standard could be a variety of crew staffing that runs the gamut from an owner occupant solo act to an outfit of multiple crews of seasonal college kids who show up every fourth day if it isn't raining. Since every painter does it his own way, if you happen to talk to two who are alike, all of a sudden, who knows? Industry standard might be a semi-trained pack of monkeys in painter's pants.

It's a whole lot different for me showing up after the sales calls of a couple of painters who figure the job at $ 40- $50 per hour and plan to do a complete job, than it is to show up after a couple of monkey handlers charging $20. Believe it or not, those who charge less by the hour usually plan to do less of a job. They don't tend to just spend less time, but the quality of what they do is even less. Those who charge more usually have some integrity about themselves . Industry standard, then, winds up being whatever the homeowner thinks is right, usually based on whomever he or she has spoken to about the job. In a word, then, there is NO objective industry standard for residential painting.

Often times where the sales call falls in the sequence of the estimates received by a homeowner is important. I always like to be the last bidder. When I can, I arrange to estimate the job after everyone else has gone first. That way homeowners can compare in the moment everything I say to the others; and I can respond to everything anyone else has said. Since I tend to know more about residential painting than most other painters, it isn't hard coming up with a better sounding painting story.

I had a lawyer friend tell me that he really enjoyed court room work because he knew the law and most other lawyers didn't. And not because of a brilliant legal mind, but rather just his more complete knowledge led him to frequent victory. Using my educational approach to sales presentation coupled with a very complete body of knowledge, I often educate homeowners into the only answer possible: to hire me and my approach.

Can you imagine trying to hang a picture with a thumb-tack on a dirt wall? Would you ever try to build a house on top of a rotten basement foundation? Yet, some people expect that paint will stick to an equivalent paint foundation.

People talk about how well paint will adhere, how well-bonded it is. The truth is any paint is well-bonding and will adhere to what it dries on. The problem is what it dries on is sometimes itself not attached to the house.

Not that we need get into a philosophical debate, but what IS the house? If we want the paint to attach to the house, we had better realize what it is and what it isn't. Because if we attach the paint to what is not the house, obviously a parting of the ways will be inevitable: peeling paint!

As a paint job ages, not only does the exposed paint deteriorate but also the under-layers of paint and the outer layers of the underneath wood it attaches to. I have seen bottom layers of paint reduced to chalk, scale and even mere powder. Sometimes it looks like it is disintegrating. It is such a thin layer of wisp that it is hard to believe it may once have been a proud, tough, protective paint film. Old soldiers may never die, but old paint will as well fade away. You might think this details the entire process of paint failure, but it leaves out disintegration of the outer wood layer to which the bottom paint layer is attached.

As the paint job ages, so does the wood of the house. The constant wet-dry cycles, with the continual passage of moisture in and out of the house walls, along with the ongoing beating of heat and cold, cause considerable suffering to the exterior wood surfaces. As that wood rolls with the punches of all of the moisture and temperature abuse, the outer layer of its surface expands and contracts, eventually vibrating itself loose from the grabbing layer of primer paint. Like taking a potted plant and shaking it where the roots of the plant become loose, so too the bonding layer of paint is vibrated free from the wood that holds it. This loosening of the point of attachment of the primer layer makes room for further degrading action.

With that space now microscopically tilled, moisture will begin to have its way with the wood fiber. Passing through the wood fibers, first microscopically wetting and then usually drying, this repetitive wetting-drying erodes the outer-most layer of the wood into dust. Like the desert arroyos that several times a year channel great volumes of rainy season drainage, the outer wood layer is itself rendered to dust during its dry seasons. It becomes comprised of particles of wood fiber that are no longer attached to the wood core of the cedar siding or pine trim. It becomes a community of hermit fibers no longer attached to the society of wood. Divided, these independent pockets of fiber have not the strength to withstand the onslaught of time and weather to effectively bridge the paint to the integrity of the solid wood of the house. That is when the paint falls off. We call it peeling. And in truth, what had been the house has now deteriorated into unattached old-wood-fiber, now rendering the house microscopically reduced in dimension, thus adding data to the what-is the-house- debate.

It stands to logical reason that any paint attached to this dusty layer, even if well bonded to it, will fall off along with that dust. Any paint job of integrity MUST include the removal of such a faulty layer. Most do not, mine do. This fact keeps me in business. My sales education job is to impart this to prospects. The better I do that the more work I get.

It is true that those who can, do; those who can't, teach. There is the business corollary, where there is a fundamental difference between doing and talking, job performance and sales talk. How many times has a salesman promised something that you never receive? What sun or moon does an over-eager, or unscrupulous, salesman not promise during the sale's job? There is probably more misrepresentation of intention at the point of sale than during courtship when he tells her he loves her.

I am in the painting business, but I tell my guys that we are in the show business, the "painting show ". The first act of this show is the sales routine. It's as though I give the first act for free, and to find out how it ends you have to buy the ticket. The strength of my opening act is largely the volume of very detailed information I throw at prospects. Is it true? Is it accurate information? No one can say with absolute certainty, although I believe it all to be 100% true. It nonetheless sounds reasonable enough often enough, and that's what sells tickets.

I call them stories but they are all supported by experience. When I tell the story about wood fibers eroding in the constant wet-dry cycle, people line up for front row seats. When I tell the one about the problems of other painting contractors' packs of monkeys climbing all over their house, they buy my ticket. It is really just so much story telling; whatever they choose to believe is their reality. Sometimes you can actually communicate with someone. Sometimes you only talk at them. Like lemmings at the cliff, they will follow their preformed beliefs without distraction.

I once did a job for lady who deemed herself an artist. She knew exactly what she wanted for colors and gave me their names. She was quite thorough, but only in her own mind. She thought she was leaving no room for pilot error in the selection of the paint color. What she didn't take into account was that the manufacturer had reformulated the color that went with that color name. She supplied the color name, but the manufacturer at that time connected that name with a different color than the one the customer had previously used.

Previously, when you requested Cape Cod Gray, you received the color she expected. Sometime after her previous paint job, the manufacturer began to make the paint that went with that name with more blue in it. Same name, different color. When I came with the current Cape Cod Gray paint and began to put it on, she put a quick halt to the operation accusing me of cheating her with a color switch subterfuge. As if it mattered to me what color I put on her house! But that is what she believed. It took quite a bit of negotiating at that point for me to continue for her. But it was clearly not my responsibility. In effect, she was accountable for color name selection, not me. She could take up with the manufacturer what colorant they put into paint carrying that color name!

Eventually, after much discussion she allowed me to continue. I finished the job and she was satisfied with my workmanship. The job came out well from my perspective, as well. It looked good, was technically well done and I made my money. But she never used me again.

I met her some time later at the local paint store. After talking a few minutes, she explained why she couldn't use me and her great satisfaction with her new painter. She made up her mind that she didn't trust me to do what she wanted, even though I followed her directions to the letter. Somehow I should have known what she wanted, not what she said. In addition to being a painter, in the painting show business, I should also have been a mind reader!

And her new painter? He is a known local shyster, who has more crews on the road working for him than he can count, and in fact doesn't even know the painters on any given job. He is known throughout the local painting scene as being a cut-throat cheat and is well known for his typically short-lived paint jobs. His routine is well known to include two visits to his clients: he shows up once at the sale and again to pick up the check, with some unknown bunch of people appearing after his sales call who somehow justify his showing up the second time to collect. He is the classic trades' slob who is here to make the rest of us look good. Go figure, she likes him! He with his golden tongue has told the right story, put on the right show. To her, he is the man. And that's all there is to it.

Once a home owner makes up his mind about you, everything you do after fits into that mold. A contractor defines himself to the customer in two ways: by the image he presents and by the image the customer sees, not always the same thing. Once that image is formed in the customer's mind that is what the contractor is and will forever be for the customer. I was blindsided by this customer's blame regarding her idea of the color and the manufacturer's alteration of that particular name's color. She defined me as a bum and that was all there was to it. I have made some adjustments in my routine.

I am perfectly disciplined about the first day on a new job, for instance. For not only does the successful sales routine motivate them to buy the painting ticket, the first day on the job defines to the customer who I am and how the crew is. If we come in deliberately, organized, neat, thorough and hardworking, that's what and who we become for them. If the crew deteriorates to a pack of monkeys after that, it's ok. We have already been stamped professional.

The typical first day is filled with ceremony. I arrive first and then the crew, who know to park on the road, out of the way, never in front of the mail box or a driveway. Their approach to the house can be a little rough, though. As with most trades' crews, the typical suburban home owner sees them in the yard and immediately experiences the impulse to dial 911 for assistance: some of my guys have been rough looking if professional acting. Before introductions, my professional acting help will typically walk around for the ceremonial "viewing of the house". This is always a solemn event comprised of the behavior of professional-looking assessment. This always looks good.

The unpacking of the truck is my version of the Japanese Tea Ceremony. The mere act of opening the several doors to the storage area can alone inspire awe. I see in most home owners' eyes the same deep questioning at this point of the ceremony,
 "How in the hell does he get all of that in there?" The unpacking follows a certain order, with each of the crew filling in to make this an impressive choreograph. We set up the garage space in our "desk top", with drop cloths, ladders, paint, tools and supplies laid out in such an order you would think we had been working out of this space for months. Everything winds up in its spot, and there is a spot for everything.

We are diligent and disciplined to put things in their spot and to return things to their proper spot. Each speck of dust is removed from where it doesn't belong and every tool or supply is placed as if with Dewey-decimal system organization in its home. All of this is done until something happens. We continue this act of librarian organization until the homeowner sees it and takes notice. Once they do that, once they see that is what we do, once we become the professionals who do this, then we don't have to any more. They already know who and what we are.

At that point, the neat order of tools and supplies can become a pile of painting junk. Where once there were neat and separate arrangements of painting tools, now there will be a tossed salad of brushes, scrapers and hand tools. Where before tidiness prevailed, now there will be the busy work-staging of a hardworking crew whose concerns are no longer making impressions but good headway on a typically difficult job.

Once we have made our impression of being a neat, organized professional crew, we can dispense with it to just doing our job. If that means plowing our stuff into a pile in their garage at the end of the day, at that point it's OK. Try doing that from the start, and all you will have is trouble with a customer who will only see you as a slob. This customer will always pick apart the job and they will pick you apart as a human being. If you make the impression of being a slob, you will always be one. First impressions rule, so you must always define yourself for them as you wish to be known. Then do whatever you want.

PART 3: RELATIONSHIP WITH EMPLOYEES

HIRING, THEN HANDLING: FISHING THE WILD WATERS

There is honor amongst thieves and there is a very essential integrity in the guys who have worked for me through the years. But like rust-crusted iron, the purity is sometimes deep down. Foremost in my job interview of them, I have presented the two requirements that attempt to lay the groundwork for everything I would ask of them: first, that they wear painter's pants every day (you wouldn't think that would be too hard) and second, that they always do what they say they will do. This second rule is really the crux of my relationship with them and it is the very character trait that makes them adequate for it. This interview is meant to select those who will be (somewhat) conscientious and trainable.

I always wanted a new guy who had not painted much before, someone who didn't already have pre-formed ideas about how to do it. Since I had a very particular way of doing almost everything, I didn't want some butthead who would proudly inform me at the interview, "Well, let's see, yeah, I know how to paint! I've painted quite a bit. I painted the back of my neighbor's house AND my mother's garage." Like buying cars, if you can afford it, you're much better off not compromising with the added wear and tear of previous miles; it's always better starting from scratch with a new one. What I really looked for was their low painting mileage along with the assessment that the guy is one who takes pride in what he does.

My job interview has always been a simple one, mostly revolving around my assessment of an applicant's pride in his own work. The first part of the interview is meant to establish how well he understands that most basic rule: to always do what he says he will do. If he seems to understand that, I talk with him further about that to determine if this is actually how he conducts himself. If I feel it is their first time out on this boat, I don't want them and they're gone right away. But if they do check out I bend their ear a bit more to dig into the nuances of the rule. I will want them to not only do what they say, but once they say it they had better do it, unless they then say differently. And if they intend to do something, I want to know about it. But if someone says he will and then says he won't, that proves him unreliable. Furthermore, none of this removes anyone from the realities of real world consequences to their decisions and behavior. But this is the stuff of honor and either a guy has it or he doesn't. I think of that 70's basketball smack: "you can't fake the funk of a nasty dunk".

My first employee was a friend. Over the first several years of doing business, my first four were good buddies. Doing business, splitting money and sharing work with good friends required unfailingly honorable business principles of fairness, honesty and peer- ness.

This first one to work for me was a good friend, although he wasn't at all a painter. He didn't have any relevant experience, but he needed work and I needed a helper. Was it a match made in heaven? In a limited, tunnel-vision world, you might say so. Beginning with that experience, I recognized the need and began to learn forthrightness and honesty in interactions with an employee.

I entered into this business with the self-definition of being a training and management expert. It just so happened that I was at that point managing and training painting behavior, with my interest being in these supervisory functions and less on the trade itself. And I took a great delight in imparting the required behavior and in refining the necessary communication for that. I was very precise in what I wanted and just as precise in how I went about asking for and demanding it. Quite naturally out of this came the rule to always do what you say you will do. For, once I turn my back on a guy, I have to have confidence he will at least follow through. What good is someone if he declares an intention and then goes off in an opposite direction?

If it's not accepted from a sled dog, why would anyone accept it from a human employee? And since I was so extremely precise about everything, in order for a helper to be useful at all he had to declare his intentions for a whole list of to-dos, along with a whole regimen of how he will do it.

Business management styles change like clothing fashions. There was management by objectives, total quality management, team building, etc. In all of these there is the bottom-line objective of getting the most out of your help as possible. There is always the manager's need to discover the hidden start button for each of the help. There is a simultaneous necessity to discover and avoid the individual hot buttons for each of them as well.

I talk over the happenings on my crew with my wife. When I relate some of the more juicy shenanigans to her, she looks at me like I'm crazy, shakes her head in disbelief and levels me with, "Just fire them all!" This may be the conventional response, but it isn't the path I follow.

I have to remember every day that this is an industry made up of guys that aren't the type that get taken home to meet someone's parents. Take a tour of paint crews in your home town and you will see this is true. Each and every one of the guys that will be hired in this industry has some aspect of dysfunction and underachievement, are typically hot-headed, otherwise unskilled and largely unprepared for living in the world. Include many trades' employers in this profile as well. It is an industry most of us fall into by default and never by design or purpose. So if one group of employees is a problem due to their bad habits, the next bunch could be worse and certainly not different. This makes a strong argument for keeping marginally troublesome employees, and it also makes the case for developing a large measure of employer tolerance for undesirable behavior.

Mark started working for me when he was 18 years old and continued until he was forty. He worked his way up through the many crews and made it to the top. He is a top performer, knows how to apply paint, and takes an interest in a good product. What more could you want? Every day I have to remember that workmanship is my focus; personal character is just excess baggage. If over-riding tolerance for the unexpected and undesirable was not staunchly in my arsenal, Mark wouldn't have been kept because he would have been the first to go when "firing them all".

I've hired a lot of guys through the years, and the pool from which I've picked them has evolved into ever wilder waters. Whereas at first I brought in friends, later I ventured out into the real world to sample the unknown. And like fishing in the ocean, when you throw your line in you have no idea what you will pull out on it, what will be attached to it.

My first helper was a friend who had painted a little during college, but wasn't at all on a professional level. I had begun my painting career with a professional painter and then put in a considerable time with another to learn what is actually known as the European Method. Not a Western addendum to the Kama Sutra, it is the collection of common painting procedures used and passed from master to apprentice throughout Europe. To allay your cognitive dissonance with this, consider that in Europe, in contrast to the US, painting is a trade of respect. In Europe, painters are not on the bottom rung of the cultural ladder, as in the US, but enjoy the status of respectability in society. They earn this with their workmanship and their workmanship follows the European Method.

My friend and first helper didn't know that system of paint application, and refused to learn it. But he more than happily replaced it with his own method. Being the stickler I am for detail, this always grated on me. But he was a friend and was really only helping me out. It quickly dawned on me that whatever he did, I most likely wouldn't have to do; it didn't matter what method he used to get there. Tolerance became my friend. Jobs were completed and I learned to see the forest without needing to focus on the trees. But it didn't stop being a threesome: him, me and my tolerance for his technique.

At some point, friend one was joined by friend two. It was then that I received the arithmetic lesson of employee management: one plus one is not always a pleasant two. The quantity and quality of the work was unreliable when they worked together. And it was up to me to decipher why, how and what to do about it.

I began to develop a management style I call mood management and social directing. I realized their workmanship was directly related to the quality of their relationship to me and how they felt about themselves doing the work. So I had to do whatever it took for each to have the impression that our relationship was just as they wished and that their workmanship was valued by me. This wasn't hard to do since we WERE good friends and their work DID meet the standards I required. But I DID make the effort to ensure their recognition of this. Consider this a form of positive reinforcement.

Abraham Lincoln is credited with identifying this social grace with the words, "Tact is the ability to describe another as they see themselves". In my case, I wanted to relate to my help in the fashion that they wished us to relate in order to minimize the roadblocks to their meeting my goal of their producing a day's work in a day's time.

Essentially, I wanted them to be in a good mood. A grumpy guy doesn't work well. Neither does a depressed one, an unhappy one or an angry one. So, it was up to me to see to it that my two guys didn't feel like that on the job.

I wanted them to be happy about their work, their boss and their co-worker. To accomplish this, I joked and clowned around all day, and they did as well. Everyone enjoyed it. It made everyone's day pass quickly and it made our dealings with each other fun. While joking around these two did not clash and they completed their assignments. Most importantly, this was accomplished through my intentional management of it. This became my foremost on-the-job management tool. As I said, I call it mood management and social directing.

I was juggling two employee balls and could afford neither to fall. Mood management and social directing came into play in much stronger ways as the years went by and the crews became larger, more unknown and much wilder.

Eventually these two friends went on their ways and I was faced with my first employee crisis. I wasn't ready for full-blown employee help-wanted advertising, but I was ready for a low-keyed one. I wanted to try posting a simple hand written note somewhere. I put it in a place that would not only have conscientious people reading it, but where they might even value it more highly for being hand written. I posted it in the local Zen Center.

I did get a response, but it wasn't exactly the one I had in mind. Fred was the fish drawn in by that bait, but I've wondered since if perhaps he was the bait and I was the fish. He was a seventeen year-old high school drop- out whose girl friend's mother was a Zen Center member. It was she who referred him to me. And although it still makes sense to have put out the call for someone conscientious who had a Zen attitude of attentiveness and kindness, I have since regretted her kindness in attentively sending him to me.

Fred's story appears elsewhere, but he was a hot and cold running tap of water for many years. He finally burned me for good and I fired his ass. It was a grand firing and my petty gratification of that moment almost made up for the years of trouble he gave me. There was a saving grace in my relationship with him, because a whole long string of employees came from him.

Even during Fred's good periods, a rare occurrence during his tenure with me, his opinions were rarely of value to me. But at one of the few such times, I brought in his good buddy Pat to work for me. It was so easy to come up with this new guy, that I've used this strategy for staffing ever since. If there is such a thing as renewable resources, it is that guys have friends or they meet new ones, and they all need a job. By just putting out the word, guys will come; and there are always guys out there who will come to work. I have used this pool of workers for thirty years and Fred's legacy continues to this day with one or two returning guys who are direct descendants of Fred.

Not that these guys were gold. Many, though, were good enough. Eventually the vein played out and I was again faced with an employee hiring crises. This time I went to the newspaper and was prepared for endless calls, bad talking rough necks, urban hip gangstas, biker type machos who would make claims they couldn't back up, as well as appointments they would not keep. I was prepared for guys who would want to come interview and to work using the bus for their transportation, even though all is in the suburbs with no bus routes. I knew there would be guys being driven by someone else because of lost licenses due to DUI. There would be old guys recently laid off from real jobs at local industry just needing to fake their way into anything. I anticipated listening through all kinds of boasts, claims and macho challenges. I wasn't disappointed.

The want ads produce the oddest collection of birds you could imagine. I had a guy claiming to be a twenty year pro who didn't know how to put up an extension ladder. I had another self-described seasoned pro inform me he didn't work with oil paint or dust. I had a guy show up with bumper stickers on his relic that made ME blush. I had a guy so desperate for the job he grabbed a grinder to show his stuff who only proceeded to put a half-inch gouge in his leg. Two years ago I had a weirdo come into work on his second day waving rock album covers around and raging about the cultural immorality the Almighty has instructed him to preach against. I had a Hells Angel type inform me he had to work on the back of the house only, because "they" were looking for him. There was another newbie who turned out to be a parole violator who really did have to stay out of view, worried about a different "they". I had a woman show up for an interview who thought she could get the job by unzipping her jacket to show off her wares. There are too many to count who had to wait for a ride from a girlfriend or neighbor. There were accents and dialects I couldn't decipher. There was oil and gas that had to be cleaned from my driveway, even cigarette butts. There is a reason fishermen don't eat what they catch from the canal waters. There is a reason I don't want to go to the paper for help. But you do what you gotta do.

One thing was for certain, the pool from which I fished served up the same kind of fish. If one guy was unreliable, unskilled, bad tempered or just plain rough, the next might be a whole lot more so. If one guy was hard to handle, the next is just as likely to be worse and certainly not different.

There was one simple fact. However bad an individual guy was, the next would be the same or worse. So, it behooved me to learn to deal with them. I was a mechanic working with broken tools, and it was my job to learn how to use them.

In order to survive and even thrive in this business, I have had to practice the patience of a priest on prison duty. Guys are wild animals who choose or choose not to go along at any moment of the day. The negotiation for this peace process is continual and ongoing. For, in any given moment, they're as likely to paint as fight; as likely to paint well as work carelessly; as likely to get along with each other as plan a crewmate's painful encounter.

Guys are nuts. It's not like you are dealing with well put together accomplished gentlemen. You can count on something, though. You can count on them being unpredictable. You never know what they will do next, making real the feeling of the one armed paperhanger. In this case it is like handling a bunch of loose cannons rolling around on deck. You never really know what anyone is going to do next.

Essentially what you have is a bunch of unskilled, socially unprepared, scared young men (i.e. old boys). From the pool these guys come, you'd be naive to expect more. You'd be real disappointed if you had high expectations. As a matter of fact, to survive at all, you must not only have but maintain low character expectations. It's not that I expect the worst from them. But if I only expect little, I can constantly work to obtain what I want.

I have one guy who will be starting, I assume, his twenty-first year with me next season. He is reliably a very good painter, but he is off the bottom of the chart with social graces with the other guys. Even HE shakes his head and grumbles about the leniency I show toward the others, even though he has enjoyed twenty years of strategic kindness from me. I believe I take a very unique approach to production management.

From his point of view, to him I "show understanding" or respect, but to the others I show spineless groveling. Therein lays the enlightened fact: like baby robins in the nest, they all sing the words of the same tune, "Feed ME! ME! ME!"

One of the first lessons I learned is that managing these guys is a lot like swimming. When you stop you sink. I really do love them all, and have felt fondness for everyone who has ever worked for me. But in this one way, they are disappointing.

Have you ever watched a driver with a team of horses or dog-sled mushers with their leashed animals? Even though they're leashed and the driver has a whip, he nonetheless needs constantly to provide his motivational speeches to keep them going. And with my guys, if I cease mood managing, they will inevitably fall back into their own dysfunctional behavior patterns.

What does their dysfunction look like? That their workmanship suffers is the first sign, although it may not be the most obvious if it's three floors up. Maybe he or they take a lot of breaks; or they show the tell-tale stand-around-with-that-hanging-head- look. Then there is the walk back and forth to the tool truck for the just one more piece of equipment stratagem. Or maybe he just acts like he's in a bad mood. Maybe he's only in a bad mood with one other guy, maybe that other guy is me. Maybe he masks his anger in deep-cutting innuendo. Maybe he throws off that mask with a well-placed punch or in a strategically tossed bucket of paint. And then there are the excuses, "explanations" about production quality. There is the classic "I didn't do it ", or it's alternative, "I thought it was already done " or " It was someone else ". They might show up late saying, " sorry I'm late, I ran out of gas", " I'm sick(read hung-over)", " couldn't raise bail", "someone stole my license plates" (actually proudly declared to me) . With regards to yesterday, "I couldn't come in because my painter pants were still wet from washing", " I hate so and so (on the crew)", "my girlfriend died!" (actually only her faithfulness to him).

But despite the nonsense of these kinds of excuses and attitudes, when all of the spitting and stamping is done, these guys are dynamite workers. If you want to work with them, you have to deal with the thorns of their roses.

I realize that what I want from them is their production behavior. Everything else is, more or less, secondary. As long as they produce, as long as they don't interfere with the others producing or with me managing them to produce, all is well. But it's like what I imagine it would been like standing in a shit storm: you're better off, much better off, not facing into it.

I had a guy work for me near the beginning of my business years that started with me when he was just seventeen. He is the fish who wound up on my line with the job announcement at the local Zen center, which ought to have attracted a conscientious, hardworking, wholesome person. Instead I got the rat known as Fred.

Fred was a seventeen year-old high school drop-out. But in addition to his youth, his lack of painting skills and life skills in general, his resume included the additional fact of his having recently been released from jail. So, he was not only young, inexperienced and un-conscientious, and he wasn't just unwholesome, but he was an *actual* thief. And over the course of ten years of on and off employment, he flip-flopped back and forth from good to bad behavior. He worked well one day, and lied and cheated the next. In essence, he stole time for pay. At the end of his tenure with me, after a long ten year management battle, I finally caught wind of his stealing from customers as well. Fred was my case study in management style development. And everything that could go wrong did.

In the beginning, Fred was an eager enough kid who wanted to learn to paint. Or maybe he just wanted a pay check. But it soon became very clear that he derived affirmation from approval by me. Opportunity for advancing skills, increasing pay and responsibility were all necessary to him. But my approval, acceptance and inclusion of him were what made his motor run. How sad, that in the course of time, the dirty side of Fred's own character caught up to him and not even his deep need for an empowering relationship with me could keep him from disintegrating.

If acquiring his engagement in matters painting was the goal, his complaining or excuse-making were disregarded. I could obtain his commitment through the combined use of instruction, side by side working and the inevitable, incredible, master-apprentice type bond that comes from that. And in that manner, two years went by wherein he alternatively bitched and made excuses, and learned and displayed some developing painting skills. In the middle of the second year, disaster struck that put an end to that. He was in a motorcycle crash. But having his body wrecked was less damaging than was his misuse of the rather large insurance settlement that he received.

I didn't see him for several years, other than when I brought him a couple of Playboys and Penthouses while he was in traction. I guess I wanted to remind him of something more important than being messed up in the hospital. He, though, had something totally different in mind. When he finally left on his own foot power, bolstered by the large amount of insurance settlement money, which amounted to an alternative kind of empowerment, Fred went on a spending spree. He bought cars and other cool stuff, like drugs. He liked crack cocaine and he used a lot of it.

Crack is more than a drug, it is a lifestyle. To understand what it does to a person, you have to see that for the user it occupies a level of importance beyond that of religion or marriage. Forget about any Judeo-Christian values. Think "RAT"!

To put it into some perspective, I had another guy once confess to me that his ex-wife was no longer in his life because, "now, the crack-pipe is my wife." I shudder at the memory of those words. Fred's deterioration was to become just this ugly.

After a time he returned to work for me, but he wasn't the same old Fred. I was still practicing my "bottom-line" management style of acceptance through mood management, but somehow things were not working out with him. I knew he knew HOW to paint, but his work was often not coming out well. His attitude was frequently cranky and disagreeable, and he began to miss days at work. After a long time even my naiveté had to give way to a new thought: "Oh, this was no longer Fred, it was the cocaine speaking for him". He was still using the stuff and it made him a truly despicable character.

Everyone who knew our situation earlier had praised the father-son quality of our relationship. There was praise regarding the positive attributes Fred had actually shown, how good this job was for him. I, of course, nonchalantly agreed, while privately patting myself on the back. But all had changed with us; it now taking on the flavor of spoiled meat on a tasty bun.

Over the course of ten years, Fred was let go or left unannounced many times, only to come back a year or so afterward promising to make good. Finally, he broke the camel's back and I sent him away for good.

It seems that in addition to developing quite a taste for crack cocaine, he never really got rid of the stickiness on his fingers nor was he able to overcome the despicableness of his own dirty need to step on toes, lie and cheat as well as steal. In my tunnel vision world, I never discovered his stealing from customers' homes until the very end of his time with me. But when it did all come into focus, there was a trail of theft in his wake.

Sometime during his second year, Fred was left alone on a job for a few hours with another worker. That night the home owner accused me of having stolen a necklace. I self-righteously denied this, completely believing neither I nor either of the guys had even been in the house. Checking this out with the two of them confirmed this, until in private, much later, the other employee admitted Fred HAD entered the house to "use the bathroom". After confronting him, Fred adamantly denied his guilt. It wasn't until much later that the real meaning of an "accident" occurred to me: Fred had "accidentally" poured a gallon of paint thinner on the driveway, dissolving the binder in the hard blacktop, effectively creating a four foot by four foot soup of permanently liquid blacktop. This unfortunate development thankfully killed any further discussion of necklaces, but did raise the issue of a ten thousand dollar driveway, the homeowner's dislike of the paint job anyway, and ended with his advice that I should just take payment and get the hell out. I eagerly accepted and couldn't leave quickly enough.

Fred made a bad habit of stealing from jobs that was sometimes not even very well hidden, just not proven. Once, in the delightful effect of his charming innocence, he had all day tried to borrow thirty bucks from one of the other four guys on the crew. He didn't care whom he got it from, he just knew that he had his eye on a bag of marijuana that would set him back that much. No one would lend him the cash, which spoke plenty about what everyone thought about him. Well, guess what?   That night the homeowner's son wound up having misplaced the curious sum of thirty dollars that had been on his dresser. Fred HAD been seen going into the house, against orders, to "open a window for painting". "Cashless" Fred became "stoned" Fred that night.

Another time he was caught red-handed by the homeowner, or maybe I should say silver-handed. She discovered him standing with a fistful of quarters next to her change collection. He thinks quickly on his feet, and declared that he needed the coins to prop open windows so they wouldn't get painted shut. I see this woman from time to time at the local paint store, and she still shakes her head over this. I feel like hanging mine.

There are other thievery stories, from the missing silverware to the burgled art collection. Some can be traced to Fred, some only point to him. But he was a really bad guy who had a last chance with me a few years ago. He came back again, promising to show his transformed self and wanting to prove himself to me. His good behavior lasted about two days, even though I kept him around for a few months.

In the course of that time his painting quality went down the toilet, and he managed to bring others with him. He skipped, missed, messed, broke and alienated his way through a bunch of jobs. All the while with my believing that I was able not only to draw good work out of him, but also assist the positive transformation in his character that I thought he supposedly wanted. He had me completely buffaloed.

At some point I could no longer deny reality. I threw him out. As I did, I made it perfectly clear to him just how low a person he was, that I never wanted to see him again. After literally making him cry, I had one of the other guys drive him home, since the loser didn't even provide his own ride. And to rub it into him, I told his driver to take his time, I would pay him his hourly wage to take out the garbage, and it would be worth it to me. And as a parting note to Fred, who was for me the first in a long list of apprentice-like young men to work for me, who had enjoyed a father-son-like relationship with me, he was not just kicked out but also warned to never come near me, my job, or my family, that if he ever appeared in my yard I would "let out the dog, call 911 and then come out the door with my 9mm." I really hated the guy. He is the only one who has worked for me for whom I ended with ill will.

What came from this experience was a different kind of keen nose for this kind of trouble, and an ever vigilant need to look after the help. Their behavior needs to be continually evaluated for the positive as well as the negative. The negative needs to be further sub-divided into either acceptable non-compliance or showing the signs of the clearly unacceptable. The latter needs to be immediately weeded out; the former needs managing. In this there are good guys who act out and bad guys who act up.

For one thing, guys require much ego-building. As their employer-manager, I am an ego-builder, mood manager and sometimes their daytime social director. It has become clearly obvious to me that guys who are in a good mood and who feel good about themselves work better. They will work better, get along better and display all of the positive, agreeable attitudes that employers desire. Otherwise they're in a bad mood and will need to express it.

I've talked with so many contractors and trades businessmen who complain about needing to "baby-sit" their help. They voice criticism of the helps' inability to manage their own lives. They hate the way these guys never come in ready to work. There is resentment expressed over the bad moods, bad attitudes, bad habits, bad manners and the basic bad character of their help. There are so many one-man, solo acts that arrive at that crew size by virtue of their inability or unwillingness to spend time and energy managing their help's mood and attitude. I had a lawyer friend who set me straight on this: they pay me the bigger bucks to take care of the headaches, if it were without headaches everyone would do it. So I make bigger bucks as a mood manager and baby sitter!

Coming from a background in Behavior Management it was natural to me to distinguish employees' behavior independent of production behavior. I understood that the display of desirable behavior of my help was directly related to how I acted. And at this late date in the development of myself as employer, I see just how necessary and far reaching this remains to be true.

I regard myself as a training and management pro. In the painting business, as in any business I'm sure, if you want to give a service product that is consistent in its level of quality, you must not only have quality servicemen, you must have the wherewithal to train them. I came into the business as a tradesman at entry- level journeyman status at best, but maintained an inquisitive and learning attitude that ultimately brought me, perhaps, to near the top of my industry. I know how to do it all so I am able to train someone based on my own experience and knowledge of what works.

Standards and procedures are continuously in need of upgrade, making continuous my need for ongoing personal learning and crew training. Maintaining a particular standard is an ongoing necessity. For when the cat is away, the mouse will play. When the manager stops looking, the quality will slip.

In the field of Behavior Analysis, we know that behavioral events are behaviors done by an individual sandwiched within the environmental conditions that precede and follow these actions. As a manager of behavior, then, I must attend to the Setting in which the target behaviors will occur and I must manage the Consequences of those behaviors that effect their performing those actions moving forward. From my entry into the business of managing employees I had the unique advantage of this highly technical method of management. If I wanted some behavior out of a guy, I knew I had to put it in and then I had to manage it.

I've hired a lot of guys in my thirty years as a painting contractor. I always tried to qualify them during an interview. My ear would always get bent listening to their extensive experience as a painter, and their self-portraits would always come framed in gold. It was always up to me to assess or decipher a new hire's skill, but sometimes I dropped the ball.

During one particularly busy summer, I had my typical heavy load of residential work, but was trying to build my business by keeping up with the additional demand of three custom home builders. At some point, I needed more help and I needed it right away. My best source of new guys continued to be acquaintances of the current help, and lucky for me there were a couple practically waiting in line.

As I recall, there was a boyfriend of a girlfriend's sister. And there was another guy that a few of them just knew from "around". They both started the next day. These two rookies entered a game in which the coach was also the quarterback who was calling plays while breathlessly making strategy and staffing decisions while running plays himself along the way. In short, I was overwhelmed with job assignments, quality control and applying paint myself. I didn't have time to indoctrinate these two, and was unable to show them what I wanted or more importantly how. I just set them upon a simple task and then took my eyes off of them while I went about my own production tasks.

I thought if they did it together, chances were better that AT LEAST ONE of their four eyes would be open at any given moment, and not too much damage would happen. The closets in the new house needed painting. And they are typically out of view, in low light and therefore tolerant of a lower standard than a living room wall. Perfect!?

I was busy calling plays and throwing passes throughout the morning, so it wasn't until midday that I had the chance to look over the progress. And progress there clearly was, just that it was more comedic than dramatic.

Much paint had been used and most of the closets had paint in them. Unfortunately, most of that paint walked out of the closets on the hands, faces and clothes of the two rookies. And the paint that was actually applied was smeared around unevenly on the walls and dripped and spilled on the floor. The closets looked more like a kindergarten play station than the object of a professional painter's attention.

Perhaps you could have made a case for the interior of the wall spaces being somewhat well covered, but nowhere were corners painted. These two had rolled paint on the ceiling and wall spaces without bringing the paint completely into the corners. These areas had a border of unpainted drywall rimming around a center of painted space. They later told me they didn't think it would show…

In addition, they had short-stepped the material-preparation stage of their little painting project. They poured the paint directly into their paint trays without the, apparently unneeded, time consuming step of stirring it first. The paint had been delivered a week or so prior to their painting, so it was clearly bottom heavy. The result was a marbleized color swirl of liquid that dried on the walls to a decidedly unacceptable multicolored rendering.

The painted walls almost screamed "stupid!" The topography of it gave the impression of a relief map. In Braille, it might have contained a message I didn't want to know. It had to be sanded smooth and painted. In good conscience and technically speaking, we can't say it was "re-"painted.

One of these two rookies, it turned out, was the neighborhood idiot. You know the type. When you passed him in school or on the street you punched him for no reason. And like some real life Bozo clown, he just swung himself upright and continued on his way as if he didn't feel it. He continued on as if this was what was supposed to happen. Dumb AND unfazed was an unattractive combination to me.

This one was fired on the spot. It was when he looked at me and in earnest asked me what I thought of his work. It was when he actually believed I would give him a passing grade. It was when he displayed he didn't have even a clue. The words are famous with me now, "So, Mike, wuddayuh think uh muh work? Yuk, Yuk". I couldn't eject him fast enough!

The other one was different. For some reason I wanted to keep him, even though he had the blanked out demeanor of a teenager who smoked too much marijuana. His social skills and work habits seemed to portray some zombie-like persona, but I detected someone decent within, and again, for some reason I liked him. Soon though, I realized the reason for his behavior. He WAS a blanked out teenager who smoked too much marijuana. But I liked him and worked with him. He caught on, learned, improved, and twenty years later he still works for me. I think quite a bit of him as a painter and as a man. Mark is one of the real success stories in the lives of my help.

To this day, when someone does one of those patently stupid things, this guy or I will look over to the other and repeat," So, what do you think of *muh* work now? Yuk, yuk".

It certainly wasn't a bed of roses with this guy, even if he turned out mostly OK. It has been like pulling teeth with him, and I'm still handling him with kid gloves. I never stop mood- managing anyone whom I depend on for doing a job, and he no less than anyone. With all of them, I take responsibility for their performance as well as their attitude. I look after them like a mother hen. I just don't let them know it.

There are many ways of doing this, but all of them depend on just keeping an eye on them. And as I said before, if you want a behavior out of a guy, you have to put it in and then you have to manage it. Sometimes what seems simple and straightforward isn't.

Soon after the closet episode, I resolved to give more attention to Mark. In traditional apprenticeships in painting, apprentices are given very menial tasks. By mastering simple and somewhat inconsequential skills, the apprentice-rookie can develop good basic skills and work habits. But this was the1980's and not the 1880's. This guy was going to make me money or he was going to have to pay me. So I had to find something real for him to do.

There was a sanding task. It involved a complicated stained wood stair system, with wood steps, risers and stringers complete with a full handrail including the posts and spindles. One of my other guys had completed the staining and first coat of varnish, and the system was ready for a light sanding to take off the raised grain and to make everything smooth to the touch before the next coat of varnish.

I was proud of myself for devising a traditional apprentice-like job for this new guy. He would learn how to do a simple, but universal, step in an important process. And along the way, he could learn something about the necessary attitude of a painter, the requirement for continuous attention for evaluation. He would have to lightly sand the outer surface of the varnish layer, which sits on top of the stain layer, which has penetrated into the wood and raised the grain of the wood to an unacceptable, slightly rough surface.

I thought this would be an easy, productive, yet instructive task. Driving a car is also easy, but not if you fail to use the brakes. And Mark's sanding job went like a car with the accelerator stuck. He sanded and sanded. And you can guess the result.

I saw the reason you don't turn loose a teenage burnout, dulled by too much marijuana. He sanded, alright. He sanded off the raised grain, the varnish and some uneven amount of stain that varied from spot to spot. Oh yeah, he sanded! He got a little happy with his sanding and fell asleep to it. I imagine as his inner light of consciousness went out, that little hand of his ran back and forth on auto pilot until I came along and screamed him out of his rubbing nirvana.

"Whu? Huh? What do you mean?" were the sounds coming out of his half-awake (half-asleep!) face. I'm sure he thought he was really trying. He must have thought he was doing it right. More accurately, when his awareness left the control room of his mind for places unknown, I'm sure the parting words to his hands were, "Don't forget, do a good job!" He was a goner when I came to him, his hands ablaze with rub-a-dub-dub, and the fix for his handiwork was lengthy, expensive and needed to be done in secret.

In truth, you could easily say the stair system was ruined for staining! About all it was really good for was painting because once it had had the stain so unevenly removed, it was impossible to make it even again. But I was being paid to stain not paint, so I had to do something, and I had to do it in a way that the builder didn't catch wind of.

The only thing I could do was have one of the experienced guys spend time spot staining, judiciously putting studied amounts of stain of varying colors in different areas to try to give an appearance of acceptability. He must have spent a day or so doing it, all the while the rest of us keeping vigilance for fear the builder would show up.

The final result was a spotty, smudged, uneven stain job that consisted of multiple layers of stain of varying custom colors. It wasn't all that noticeable, if you weren't looking at it. Or as they say, you wouldn't see it from atop a fast horse! But a painter would look at it and know something was off, even if he didn't know exactly what. He would see the unevenness that would cause him to step close and examine the job.

If he were me, he would step up, remove his glasses and practically touch his nose to the wood for a real close look. He would look around and discover the dark and not so dark areas. He would see variations of color and smudges of color that didn't make sense. He would realize it didn't make any sense because it would look like someone had applied stain over the stain and then over that, smudging colors into a very indistinct but nonetheless almost wood-like look. It wouldn't make sense because nobody would do that.

But we would and we had. I had given a task to someone who hadn't been properly trained. I had violated one of my basic management principles. I had expected behavior out of him that I hadn't put in him. And I hadn't looked after his attempts in order to provide ongoing correction of his doing it. I didn't take the time to watch until he could do it properly on his own and I didn't check his progress at intervals frequently enough to avoid this major, almost complete meltdown.

This was my expensive house-part-wood-finishing-Chernobyl, and the bottom line was it was entirely my fault. The buck traveled and stopped here. And this was the lesson: if I think a task is small and unimportant, think again.

MY KIND OF GUY

Is there good and bad? Is someone either a good guy or bad guy? Are there good workers and bad? I have always tried to qualify a prospective new hire and have used many different methods and various interview techniques. I might as well incant eeny meeny!

I brought a friend on board first. And then another. And another. These were either my best friend or a very good one. When I ran out of indigent friends, willing to work that is, I tried the note at the Zen Center. It was an attempt to attract a better qualified candidate. But as the story went, it only attracted a better qualified note reader. The candidate himself was a bum, a realization to emerge much later. I tried the want ads, but that was fishing in a toilet. I knew I didn't want to do all of the painting myself and I also knew I couldn't generate enough income on the back of my own personal labor. It was clear I needed employees and they weren't appearing when I whistled. I finally hit upon the source of new hires.

In 1980 or so, I hired the rat known as Fred. He had a friend, Pat, who I hired. They had a friend Carl who came on board. Then Carl's friend Aaron. Then Carl's brother Bubba. After Bubba there was Earl and then Alphonse. Then came Mark, Bubba's wife's sister's boyfriend. And of course the bozo clown from the closet painting episode. From Mark came Kyle, AJ, Clem, and Tom. Along the way there were a bunch of guys who just didn't make the grade, lasting just a few days. This line of succession continued until the spring of 2003. It was a good run. But apparently even that line ran out of indigent friends willing to work. At that point I went to the newspaper and a new line has developed. The point being, current help will almost always know guys who want to work.

Not every guy who shows up works out, and I have developed certain criteria to look for in the ones who do. It's more of an art than even a loose science. I like to think I am methodical and strategic, but most of the time I just need bodies on the job right away, and a willingness to show up for duty is all that qualifies them. But in the ideal world I pretend to inhabit, I look for a few traits.

I don't care if a guy has painted before. If he is inexperienced, I can train him to do it my way. If he is experienced, I can at least hope to make adjustments in his procedures. Painting really is skilled labor and it matters how things are done, in what order and with what tools. Add to that the team character of my approach to crew painting and there is a lot idiosyncratic to my method. Some guys are just too ruled by the habit of how they have always done it and refuse to adopt my way. They don't get to play on my team.

Despite all that I have just said, there is one necessary trait I look for in guys. After visually checking someone over for the necessary number and function of limbs, I take the probe a little deeper. In the course of the so-called interview I just talk with him about himself and his experience, and myself and what I do. I give him a chance to talk wherein I look for signs of his pride in himself. I need a guy who takes pride in what he does. I need a guy whose self-worth is directly tied to the product of his own labor. You can't teach that. Without that he can't do what I want. Either he has it or he doesn't.

A guy like that will observe the demonstration of a procedure and will automatically want to be able to do it. This is damned convenient! I can actually watch him try to learn it. The first time I show a newbie a given procedure I can tell if he has this basic finisher's attitude.

In the trades, there are roughing procedures and finishing ones. A house framer is a rougher. A plumber is a rougher. This is no judgment about their skill; they might be master craftsmen with master craft skills. It's just that their work does not show when the job is finished. Their work is buried under someone else's. Theirs is rough work. The finish work is what covers it. Rough work does not show. Finish work shows.

A trim carpenter's work shows. His is finish work. A tile guy does finish work, and so also does the painter. Framers and even drywall guys in new construction rely on the finishing skills of the painter. A good painter-finisher will make everyone who comes before him look good. He can fix up all of their mistakes. The vice versa also holds true; he could be a poor finisher and make the previous work look bad. All of my work is finish work and my guys must have that finisher's pride.

In ball sports, the best athletes are the ones who want the ball in their hands when the game is on the line. They are finishers. That's what I'm looking for! The finisher knows and wants his work to show and his attitude while working has a particular characteristic about it. It is having attention while doing and in Zen circles it is called beginner's mind or Zen mind. Sometimes a painter will exhibit this. Sometimes he will not. I need my guys to be that kind of finisher. They must have that kind of attention for ongoing assessment. That is what I look for in the new ones, but sometimes even a good horse throws a shoe.

Guys who have been onboard with me for a while are ones who have shown that finisher's attitude. But just because they have it doesn't mean I will get it. Murphy "don't have nothin..." on the antics of my crews through the years! Even good guys can be just going through the motions without using much critical attention. They might actually be trying, but clearly missing the boat. They can make mistakes and have accidents. They can get angry and show it. None of this is game-winning ball handling. You never know what to expect.

Sometimes the finisher's attitude goes too far and the guy thinks he is the star of the team, when all that is needed is a water -boy. The last thing I need is a Picasso up on a ladder.

I know who the top stud on the team is and there can really only be one of them, although everyone needs to be very good at what they do. I am personally a very careful and skilled tradesman. I have come to understand how to handle different fluids and coatings and the different tools used in the decorating profession and even find pleasure in their application and use. But I don't relate to the minute by minute production necessary to be an on-line painter. I find it much more pleasant to devoting myself to the perfect front door while the guys are making the money painting the house. I make the door my statement, my seal of excellence, as the top painter on the crew.

Guys will always develop superiority complexes with regards to each other and even me. This is the finisher's attitude on ego trip. If not for the periodic display of excellence of my door painting, it would be necessary for me to jump into the trenches with them and paint the side of the house (God forbid!). It is necessary for me to maintain top dog status in order to keep control of the crew.

During a typical peeling paint prep day, the guys were "having at" the house with the paint grinders. Everyone was blowing paint off the house creating quite a dust and chip storm. If creating a statue is merely removing all the extraneous marble that isn't your finished figure, grinding failed paint off the house is just removing all but the stable sub-layers under the peeling paint. But as the big league slugger needs to be in the moment, so does the paint grinder.

Seth had the task of preparing the peak of the house which included a wooden air vent at the forty foot level. I assigned him that task way up there because he was new. I thought I was being smart, but I proceeded to do just the opposite of what smart would do: I lost my attention for what he was doing. His attention was ultimately discovered to have been also seriously AWOL.

When he came back to earth to report in, his handy-work was discovered. He had prepared his area and ground off the loose paint, but he had sanded into the vent more than a little bit. He had dug into the wood of it, a serious no-no. He had removed the contoured slopes of the louvers of the vent by grinding the face of it flat. Essentially, he had transformed a louvered vent into a fixed lattice structure up in the peak of the house. It took some careful, fancy grinding to reshape what wood was left into a vent-like piece. It was necessary for me to use in myself what the new guy had disregarded: I used the finisher's attitude. It is this attention for detail, the finisher's attention, which must accompany everything a painter does. In a very basic way, some guys have it and some don't. However, whether someone has it or not, there is one piece of management I must never fail to perform: A piece of behavior may or may not be "in" a guy but I must always monitor his performing it.

END OF YEAR: PRIMING THE PUMP

If there is something to fret about, it is the continued desire of my help to work for me. They are my most important stock in trade. Since I follow a seasonal schedule, I let them all go every year at the end of the season. Their returning to work for me in the spring is a major priority. Their return, though, begins for me in the fall, before I release them for the winter. I measure their likelihood of returning by the attitude they have at the end of the season about their job, about me and about the crew. Like the conscientious farmer, I prepare the soil of their attitude in advance of the long fallow winter. I want them leaving with the wish to return. My painting show includes the audience of my help and I want the curtain to come down with them wanting more.

The first thing I do is sweeten the deal with their pay. Since there is no real industry pay standard, I can pay a guy whatever I wish. And since there is such a wide differential between pay rates that can still be profitable for me and those that cannot, giving raises is always a possibility.

If a guy is valuable, I give him a raise immediately before the final week. I also bait him with my return policy: the signing bonus upon his return. Sometimes I offer another raise upon returning. And really! A fifty cent an hour raise is almost unnoticeable to me at the end of a busy painting week. Would you care about twenty bucks a week if your business was running smoothly and profitably?

I have even offered straight up money. Once I offered an actual bonus, to be paid out after a certain number of weeks of the following season, in increments by the week. This might bring a guy back and keep him on the job. If more money isn't enough to bring a guy back then he doesn't have the right attitude about what he is doing and I don't want him anyway. Some guys are like small fish on the line. Once you reel them in their use is done and you just let them go. I usually have a few catch and releases every year. But there are keepers.

This painting show works because the guys can play their parts. The better they do that, the better the show. By the end of a season guys are at their best and I let them know. I give them positive performance reviews. I give them more responsibility and display my trust in them. This treatment can draw them in like water down a pulled drain. Their response to it is a measure of who is likely to return and gives me a heads-up on the next season's staffing.

These typically are guys who have done nothing with their lives, have prepared nothing for themselves and who have not much in the way of prospects for them. Now, all of a sudden, I am giving them stature. They have learned to be productive members of a highly skilled outfit of elite house painters. Some of the guys love that. I love the ones who do and it is those ones who do return. But it doesn't happen without my manipulations. I act to maximize the probability of their return and it is time well spent.

The other main business necessity is the spring-time ritual to get jobs. My most important method of business acquisition is answering my phone. Believe it or not, it just rings. It's like magic. Maybe it is magic. But it does ring, and I assume it does not from magic but from my hard work over the years. I take care of my customers and make sure to bring the curtain down on the painting show at their house with them clapping, because I know it is just a matter of time before they will need it again. One paint job isn't enough for me; I am looking for the repeat customer.

I keep in touch with customers with an annual post card. I either find a photo or take one that I can attach some reminder of me. I make it up as post card and send it out to my customer list every spring. This usually results in a number of calls almost immediately. It is a useful way to prime the pump with a few jobs. These prospects are prior customers, and until the recent economic downturn I got almost all of those jobs. During these tough times people are pinching their pennies, so there is no rule about this practice either.

The other thing I do is contact my main paint supplier. The store owners are long-time business friends and it is always a reunion when I show up in the spring. They ask about my skiing escapades and I ask about their hunting. We catch each other up on our families, the price of paint, the economic forecast and the latest back room jokes. I inform them I am looking for jobs, they give the ok shrug and referrals begin. Yahoo! I'm in business.

THE JOB MAP

You wouldn't try driving across country without a map. You wouldn't try building a house without plans. But when I first got into house painting I didn't have a clue about developing a business, having a plan or even how to bid a job.

My first job estimating method would have been comical if not for the painful consequences it brought me. I think I closed one eye and with the other I looked askance through the frame of my thumbs and pointer fingers and conjured a number. I would conduct this little charade and say to myself, "hmmm, about a week", or "whew, maybe a week and half". In truth, I hadn't much of a real clue. I was in luck, though, because working for short money became a forceful teacher and I was quickly convinced to think about it.

There are a variety of ways to price painting jobs. There is square foot pricing, piece pricing, house size pricing. There is even a formula using a multiplier with the house's real estate taxes. Knowing I wanted to make a minimum amount per week, I realized that a time based pricing system was what I wanted. I knew that a time and material deal would have been ideal, but unrealistic to expect for a beginner. Therefore, I resolved to develop an hourly labor-based estimating procedure. As it turns out, my estimating procedure easily evolved into the means for not only estimating time, but also cost as well as managing production. I call this procedure my Job Map.

When I approach a potential painting job, I need to know how long it is going to take to complete it. That is in reality an unknown, since each one of my different painters works at a different pace for different operations. Add to that the uncertainty of the total requirement for any *actual* given individual house part and you are left with a lot of chin scratching. All I can do is estimate how long it would take me by myself to do. I call this Par Time. By comparing any individual's typical speed with Par Time, I can effectively estimate likely costs and production time.

Through the years I have come to be able to predict to a very high degree of accuracy how long it will take me to paint just about any house part. It doesn't matter if my time is more or less than any other professional painter, since I am figuring MY time and, therefore, my price for a job. I control job production time by comparing individual painter helpers' times to my Par Time estimates. If there is relevance in the comparison of my time to another contractor's, it is only in comparing one proposed job price estimate against the other. Interestingly, I find that my time estimates are about in line with those of other painters of my experience. But as it turns out, this objective measure is meaningless for contracting, since homeowners will choose their contractor only seemingly on the basis of cost. Those cost comparisons become moot, as the more unconscious decision determiners work their magic. Therefore, I derive some value in comparing prices with others, but the greater value is derived from the development of the Job Map which provides me with the very detailed information about the time requirements of the job being considered.

In my bag of tricks I have my collection of Par Times for all known house parts. I apply these estimates part by part as I inspect the house. Each house part Par Time Estimate is entered on the Job Map as a discrete Line Item. The complete painting time estimate for each house part is accounted for as a Line Item, as a mini-estimate of its own. Together, all of the Line Items add up to account for the painting of the entire house.

It is a menial task, but a simple one. I walk around the house recording Par Time after Par Time estimates for each house part, until arriving at a completed list of Par Time Estimates that comprises each part of the entire house. I add them up to arrive at the Par Time Estimate for the entire job. If I multiple this by my hourly or daily rate I can determine my price.

The beauty of this system is that it defines each of the parts that together add up to their sum, the total Par Time Estimate for the job. This is the Job Map that functions as a behavioral blue print. Each part of the house to be painted is allotted its time estimate and every house part is accounted for. The sum of each of these is theoretically and effectively the total time necessary to complete the paint job. This Job Map is a complete job time and work description, thus making its nature as behavioral blue print.

I've been at this long enough to know that I never want to work for less than my minimum daily rate. I don't mind making more, though. Thus enters the art of price bidding, which follows a very simple rule: How much is not too much?

When I was starting out I asked a lot of questions of everyone I met. One of my favorite lines of questioning was about how to price jobs. When I once asked the savvy industry insider, his answer seemed to be flippant. But getting as much as I can for a job has been my guiding principle ever since.

I know I want to make a daily minimum, so I can't bid less than that. However, if a certain amount of money is deemed too much, maybe I won't be awarded the job. I always adhere to the dictates of the Job Map, which leaves me with three options when a prospect informs me that my price is too much. The first is to walk away. The second option is to do the job for their price. The last is a variation of the second. I use their number, but change the Job Map. But I have to take into account that changing the map alters the route. What do I mean?

The map can be changed in two ways. One is to add or remove house parts to be painted. The other is to redefine how a particular item is to be done, thereby altering the time estimate for it.

If I remove a part, it won't take ANY time to not do it. But homeowners usually want a whole job not a partial one so that is usually not an option. What I can easily do is alter the criteria of particular Line Items on the Map. Maybe I can re-estimate certain house parts to justify shortening their Par Times while still planning to perform all of the original labor. In some instances this can be done without sacrificing the integrity of the job. In other instances, I can lower Par Time by actually planning to do less for a given house part, usually in the preparation stage. Other times you just have to whip the horses to make them go faster. Or I can do it myself. In my operation, I don't plan to include my labor in production, so adding that in can significantly increase a day's production. So right there are four ways to lower my price and still give the same or close to the same job.

My overriding goal is to earn my preferred daily rate. The point is there are a number of ways to get there. Each of the ways is a manipulation of given lines of the Job Map. Each Line Item of the Job Map can be treated independently of the rest, manipulated or not, thereby permitting meaningful alterations of the job requirements that are quantifiable and specific. I see it as a behaviorally engineered alteration. Since each line item is a prediction of actual time, the *actual* actual time is dependent upon the actual person who does it. One key production management tool is the choice of whom to assign to any given Par Time Line Item.

A few summers ago I was working with a large crew of five guys on a difficult restoration of a two hundred year old farm house. It was one of my usual operations, and my guys used paint-remover grinders to hog off vast and deep layers of old paint. This is done to "restore" the house exterior down to its original wooden construction, thereby removing the unpredictable layers of old paint. As it turns out, the weakness of ANY paint job is the old paint that is left on after preparation, upon which the new paint is added. Anywhere the new is put on over old is where it is going to peel. And unless the new stuff is put on wrong, which really is hard to do even though some actually accomplish it, the peeling will be not just the new paint but the old layer will come loose and carry the new with it. My guys were hogging off the junky old paint with a vengeance to get it down to solid wood.

This old house was resisting my ordinary tough attitude toward removing the loose and failed old coatings. It had multiple layers of some of the hardest paint I have dealt with. There was, of course, lead paint in there and quite a thickness of it. It was about a quarter of an inch thick, acting like armor doing its job protecting what was underneath it from our attempts at removing it. We had gone through a number of ninety degree days in that battle against this resistant foe and everyone was close to the end of their dirty, lead dusted, sweaty ropes.

Guys were struggling through, but one was having a particularly tough time with it. The bottom line was he was not meeting Par Time for his assignment. I needed to find something for him to do that would permit him to meet some Par Time because he wasn't close to it doing what he was doing. Guys finishing close enough to par time is what makes me money. He wasn't getting that done. The homeowner inadvertently supplied the solution.

The homeowner was a large landholding, gentleman farmer/ business owner whose wealth was limited only by the question of "how much?" He liked to pretend to have to budget his money. I had painted this man's house several times before and he always had me do half at a time, a job that was still as large as any normal house. This time he had me estimate the usual half, but he asked me to leave off a part because, as he told me, "a'hm feelin' poo-ah", in his upstate New York, out of place southern accent.

But after we were going at it, he decided to add in that part, which I did, but as a time and material extra. Since the Par Time for this is the actual time it took, it was the perfect task for my slow guy. With this assignment, his snail's pace would define his Par Time, since I could bill my hourly rate for his time worked on that part. As he labored away at his "special project", the other guys plodded along with the pre-estimated Par Times and everyone was able to achieve daily minimums.

Compiling an accurate Job Map is the key to my successful management of the whole job. Because as I said, with it I can predict how long my crew will take to do the job and I can accurately forecast profit. I can also determine my price with infinite adjustment possibilities and I can effectively manage job production. This is the map of the job. And it is formulated very simply.

The Job Map is compiled on a form as a simple list. Actually it is a list of lists. I divide the job into labor and material, each occupying its own column list. I further divide the labor into preparation and finish painting, each with its own materials column. In this way, the sheet is divided into four columns, each line labeled to identify the house part it estimates. There is a house part name, and then four columns: one for preparation, a second for its materials, a third for painting and a fourth for its materials, resulting in the four columns. There are as many rows as there are house parts. I draw this grid on a sheet of paper, inputting house part types and their respective time estimate figures as I proceed around the house while assessing the job.

I look at one side of a house at a time and try to bundle together the time estimates of all the same type of house part. Thus, I bundle all of the siding of a particular side of the house, or I bundle all of the windows or all of the overhang. Whatever type of house part there is to paint, I bundle all of them on a particular side of the house as a single Line Item, but only if they will be painted with the same paint or color. If a particular house part is to be painted a different color than other house parts of the same type on that side, I give each of the different colored parts their own row on the Job Map, forming their own Line Item. The basic criterion for determining the extent of a Line Item is whatever an individual painter can do with the same bucket of paint and tools.

I have developed an eye for accurately assessing imagined squares on the siding of a house of a size roughly equal to that square footage of siding I can paint in an hour. Looking at the side of a house, I can immediately see and add up the imagined squares to estimate time for painting the siding. I have another imagined square that estimates four hundred square feet, the amount of space a gallon of finish paint will cover. Thus I have an estimate of the paint to be used, and together have time and material for that part.

I know that an eight by eight double hung window, with two window sashes each holding eight pieces of glass, will take an hour (or so) to paint including the casing. If it is a twelve over twelve I had better allow an hour and a half. If it is a single casement window with casing it will take twenty minutes. For a double casement window I allow forty-five minutes. For a double with a fixed picture window in the middle, I allow an easy hour. There are two variables for these easy casement windows. One is the type of brushing cut line the painter is required to make against the siding with a contrasting color and the other is how much there is to paint with the window cranked open. Additional time must be allowed for these variables.

I have a standard production rate for overhangs. This house part is usually constructed within a range of standard widths, but some are unusually wide. An hour of painting will normally cover about forty feet of standard width overhang. Obviously, the wider the hang the shorter the hourly run. Painted gutters add time as well. Standard newer style seamless gutters don't add much time. But the older galvanized style, with all of the little wire hangers and supports, effectively double the time required for a given section.

I have Par Times for each and every house part and have developed adjustment variables for all of the variables I can encounter. There are preparation Par Times for each of the different house parts with the determining variable being the nature of the old paint to be removed. Some old paint, as with the two-hundred year old farm house, present extra difficulty. But you can't always know in advance.

The Job Map is an accurate, technical behavioral blueprint of the estimated time of the behavior required to paint a house. Up to a point it is quite accurate. But that point is often breached. A couple of years ago I had a referral whose business partner had used me for years. He had used me several times, as had many of his neighbors and his parents as well. I came well recommended, and the new customer even referred me to his daughter. It was a nice two for one recommendation. But there were unexpected happenings on each house that reduced each of the Job Maps to a bad bet.

The man referred to me had a house in need of a simple trim painting job, but it was covered with ivy, which needed to be removed from the window openings prior to painting. A couple of my guys went at it, yanking fistfuls of stem and leaf off the house. They began with fistfuls and eventually, as these things go, they were tearing double fistfuls in a fury of yank and throw. They were covered with the stuff and at times wrapped in it. Too bad it wasn't just plain ivy, but POISON ivy! Both guys came down with cases of it. One had it bad but the other was worse. He wound up in the hospital for a day.

In this case the unforeseen was merely just unnoticed on my part, although on the homeowner's part it was blatantly unmentioned. I had failed to examine the foliage; I didn't think poison ivy would appear in that type of setting and didn't even take notice of what it was. In fact, I had never known of a house to be COVERED with it like that, and together these two facts conspired to bring my lack of attention. Lack of attention may have been my fault, but the nice homeowner ought to have owned up before I even started. Oh! Did I mention he was a lawyer?

His daughter's house fooled me in a way that was another first. Hers looked like a regular house with a regular paint job with regular peeling. The trouble with it was regular peeling, but what it was peeling off of was not the house.

I had my guys perform my standard paint removal program. They used paint- removal grinders and attacked the old paint. Some of the guys were a bit slow in their progress, but my top guy, a fifteen year veteran, was enormously slow. Some days a guy is just off his game, so I let it go as just one of those days. But when it continued into the next and then the next day, with eventually everyone else complaining about the difficulty of the grinding, I had to give it a closer look. And when I did, I was literally dumbstruck.

The guys were removing paint, but in the process of doing so they were discovering another, unidentifiable sub-coating/layer. This was something other than paint but still not the wood of the house. This interloping, unknown coating was holding the paint. It was sandwiched between the paint and the wood of the house. The paint was being removed, but it was coming off this who-knows-what coating, and not the wood. In the process of removing paint, the guys were dislodging the unknown and unexpected coating and then being able to only partially remove it, and that with great difficulty. I felt like I had discovered a burglar on the house: I didn't know what it was but I knew it didn't belong there.

Close examination immediately confirmed the presence of something that not only shouldn't have been there, but was everywhere. It was about an eighth to a quarter inch thick layer of material something of the consistency of dried cork. Or asbestos!

I freaked at that possibility!

I showed samples of it to various "experts" who deemed it not asbestos, but no one could say what it was. But it was all over the house, covering not only the siding, but the overhangs, the trim, the window and door casings, the porch ceiling and the entire railing system. It was everywhere and the only way for it to have been there, on all of these varying contours, over the wood and under the paint, was it to have been sprayed on when there was no paint on the house. Someone had sprayed the entire house exterior with this thick layer of nobody knows what and then painted it. And they had done it when the house was new, because when we removed it we came down to bare wood. It was an original application at the time of the building of this house. When my guys removed the top layer of paint they effectively took the lid off this material. They got down into this deep interloping layer and wound up trying to remove it as additional unwanted coating material. It was not removing easily at all, and the only reasonable approach was to let it stay. But there was absolutely no way to have known this prior to spending time trying to get rid of it. The moral of this story is that while a thorough prior examination is necessary, it may not be full proof.

Due to the specificity of my Job Map, I have as detailed a description of the job labor requirement as I need for normal houses. Since most of them are normal, I try to match up a painter with a Map item that he is able do at Par Time. Meeting Par Time then becomes not only the main criterion for job assignments but in determining job training as well.

Last summer I had a new guy start with me who was totally green. Not only was he green as a painter, but as a house worker at all. As his baseline, he could perform no task that could make me money. To be useful he needed to be taught everything. I began by showing him the right way to hold and carry an extension ladder in the upright position.

As with most guys trying it the first time, he had his hands reversed and not nearly separated enough to gain leverage on that awkward piece of equipment. I showed him how to put one hand high and one low, and how to support the weight of the thing in the one and to control the balance with the other. After a couple of practice lifts he was able to carry it from one spot to another. After just five minutes, he was a useful, although limited, contributor to the bottom line.

Next I showed him how to arrange drop cloths and use plastic to cover the grass and bushes. I introduced him to cutting and stapling plastic on low overhanging roofs. And I showed him how I like the extension cords laid out, the grinders supplied and the vacuum lines set up for those machines. In that short space of time he was given a set of basic universal skills that he could perform repeatedly. None of those tasks was profitable, but each was necessary. All work assignments on my jobs are accomplished in a team manner. By having the new guy, the low-wage guy, do these set-up items, the more skilled and higher priced guys were free to address profit making line items from the Job Map. If everyone on the crew is satisfying the requirements of a given Line Item of the Job Map that is what I call productive work. That is when they are making me money. It is only during that time that I can relax.

The Job Map can be seen as the complete list of all the *uni-tasks* of the particular job. The musher wouldn't ask his dogs to pull AND decide when to sit; I likewise don't want my guys deciding anything. I want them *uni-tasking*. I want them doing one thing at a time, over and over. I call this *straight-lining*. My most important management task is to bring each of the guys to a straight line. I assume that once they begin that, they will continue. This is an extension of "always do what you say you will do" and the necessary production condition for anyone to be profitable for me. At the beginning of the day or at the transition from one operation to another is the time when I am personally most busy, since it is then that workers are not straight-lining. My goal for workers is for each to complete items from the Job Map, but it is my job to manage them so that they do. In that way I am just a simple behavior manager. I provide the settings in which I expect behavior to be performed, and I follow that with the presentation of my managed consequences, the so-called reinforcement. This is merely simple behavior management. What this means is, I am occupied at two moments of time with regards to any particular worker's attention to a Line Item: when providing directions at the start of their work on a Job Map Line Item or when it is time to provide a managed consequence during or after they finish. Paying them at the end of the week or providing drinks isn't too demanding; I am most busy when assisting and directing setup.

The first thing I do is supply my guys with the tools and materials needed for a given operation. I assist them in setting up, and I do whatever must be done SO THAT they can as quickly as possible begin the process of the particular Line Item and proceed with their real job, which is profit making. They make no money for me supplying themselves or in setting up. Performing Line Item production-behavior is the direct route to profit. This is a straight line.

I think of my guys working on a given, single operation as working in a straight line. Straight-lining is uni-tasking. It is single minded and it is repetitious. Essentially, it is doing one thing over and over again, but with the painters' attention for critical detail. I continue to assist any one of my guys until he is working effectively on his assigned straight line. Like teaching a kid to ride a two wheeler, I run along with the guy until he is pedaling on his own. At the point at which everyone is working on their own straight line, I can relax. At that point I can attend to other functions.

I look at transition from one task operation to the next as the time when a lot of money can be lost. These in-between times are the house contractor's glacial crevasse: don't step in or you will get lost!

In the transition guys will display the innate talent universal to all employees. They will waste a lot of time and then begin the next task sluggishly. It seems to me that they see transition as implied paid time off and the restart is like returning from vacation, with all of the sharing and story telling you would expect. And they will do this without fail. It is the "napkin rule" applied to the use of time: whenever he can a guy will take more than he actually needs.

The behavior of my job performance is driven by the behavior of my help. Critical junctures are where I jump in to perform my function. As the simple behavior manager, I must be ready to provide the setting or managed consequence for an employee's behavior. My job description IS to provide that direction or follow-up. My job IS to manage their behavior so that they perform their assigned tasks, that they perform the Behavior Manager's desired, targeted behavior. Other than that, I have nothing I gotta' do. But HOW that is done, well, that is the REAL art of the deal!

LEVERAGE IN MANAGEMENT: BEHAVIORAL ENGINEERING

It is true we work for the pay, but a worker needs more immediate input on a moment by moment basis in order to remain motivated. Behaviorally we know that any given behavior is supported by the consequences that follow it, and that the so-called reinforcement of a given behavior is that which is provided by a behavior manager that is observed to increase the strength of that behavior. There are any number of actions an employer can take to increase the strength of employees' work-behavior. If the criterion of a successful reinforcement is the strengthening of target behavior, we mustn't be limited to the obvious choices.

Money is useful. Certainly pay rate must be high enough, but as reinforcement to behavior it has limited use. It may get a guy in the door, so to speak, but it remains a reinforcing event that occurs only once a week, rendering it too infrequent to be used as a technical behavioral reinforcement. For a managed consequence to be a useful technical reinforcement it must be offer-able each time a behavior occurs, not just at the end of a timed series of behaviors. Don't misunderstand, though, adequate pay is vital. It is the strong, needed, opening salvo in the employer/behavior manager's ongoing barrage of management interventions. But it is just the first step in a long journey.

Years ago I had a crew I used to call the wild bunch. They each were your typical trade's worker of the time, fitting the standard profile. They were to a man (boy!) high school dropouts, formerly teenaged runaways or emancipated kids, mostly former petty thieves, mostly or future former alcoholics and definitely current recreational drug using, hard-drinking roughnecks. But they were my guys! And I needed to motivate them.

I always paid well. I understood that a guy unhappy with his pay will slog his way through a day whereas a guy who likes his pay at least won't have that to complain about. I concluded that money was motivating, but at first made the mistake of thinking more was better. I also failed to heed the difference between behavioral reinforcement and bribe.

I had a job I wanted finished by a certain day and understood from the Job Map that they could accomplish that but they would have to hustle. So, I offered them a bonus, a large bonus. My recollection is it amounted to several days extra in bonus money for their working steadily though a week or so, to be awarded if they finished by the target date. In their ordinary mode of operation they might have used those extra days, or more, to finish this job. But I wanted it done by my imposed date and I wanted to begin to train them to hustle.

They did make it under the deadline and each received his bonus. I was quite pleased by my cleverness until the next job started. The next one was an ordinary situation that I didn't feel compelled to push and you might guess their response. "Hey, man! What, no bonus?" They actually were expecting one. I guess this proves street toughs smarter than rats in a cage, because one-trial learning doesn't happen in the rat lab without special surgery or experimental drugs. Hmmmm? Did I say drugs?

They gave me a hard time about it for quite a long time. They kept looking for their extra money and I had to work to wean them. I reluctantly used the method again a few times, but by then the guys were jaded by false expectations and an equally false sense of entitlement. They either expected a bonus, acted abused when they didn't get it, or rushed the job when they were offered one, cutting quality in order to cut time spent. I knew money could be used as a motivator, but I hadn't hit upon how to use it yet

I was using money as technical behavior reinforcement, but the behavior being controlled by it was producing an inadequate result. They were finishing the job on time but were doing so with a poor quality paint job. The "contract" to merely finish on time did not specify the criteria of the finished product. In these cases the guys finished on time, but the jobs weren't really good enough. I had bribed them to go out and get a job done. I hadn't provided reinforcement for their having met the criteria of a job well done. These two are not the same animal. I knew money could be used the right way, but hadn't figured it out yet.

I reasoned that the Job Map dictated spending a given amount of time on the job and that my labor expense should merely be the product of total hours worked multiplied by the sum of all hourly wages. Since my guys were not working for a fixed amount, as subcontractors, their total pay at the end of each job was their pay rates multiplied by the time on the meter at the end of the job. It was my goal to keep that total in line with the Job Map projection.

I hit upon a variation of the big bonus that looked about the same to them and almost duplicated the fixed price advantage of a subcontract. By calculating the total number of man-days projected for a given job, I was able to determine the maximum amount I wanted to pay in labor. I promised to pay them their regular eight hour day rate for the given number of dates projected by the Job Map no matter if they finished early. This seemed a reasonable plan but it had similar results as the big bonus. I wasn't where I wanted to be with this bonus thing yet.

I was close, it only needed some adjusting, and I finally hit upon the method I still use today. I knew money was the key, because it is for me. But I couldn't offer too much or they'd get spoiled. I couldn't offer it at the start or they'd rush through the whole thing. By offering a bonus near the end of the job I accomplish several things.

The first thing is they never know when the bonus is coming. I keep them guessing, not knowing when or if I will offer the extra pay. This places them on a *variable reinforcement schedule.* Reinforcement is the pairing of target behavior with desirable consequences, thereby strengthening the doing of the target behavior. If you supply the reinforcing consequence upon every occurrence of the desired behavior this is *continuous reinforcement.* In this mode of reinforcement, the doing of the behavior Is strictly related to being reinforced EACH time. If you stop the reinforcement, the behavior stops as well.

With a *variable schedule of reinforcement* the target behavior receives its desired consequence only once in a while. This strengthens that behavior to occur WITHOUT the presentation of reinforcement, because the subject has become accustomed to doing it many times before receiving the goody. Clever, huh!

This strategy works handily as a bonus motivator. First, the contract for it is only presented near the end of the chain of behavior, that is, near the end of the job. This is key. The guys cannot know when it is coming or even if it is coming. That is what keeps them on their toes. This increases the probability that they will become habituated to performing at a high level in hopes of it being offered. When it does, it comes almost like a gift, or a reward for their good behavior. You might say it comes as a pleasing consequence of a long chain of their desired behavior. You might say it comes as an example of variable reinforcement.

It is no different than the food pellet that is delivered to a rat in the Skinner box, but only after it has pushed down the bar many times. The animal never knows when it will come, but he has to perform the behavior over and over until the pellet comes. For the guys on the painting crew, they must work hard, fast and correctly. But the big reinforcement, the bonus, only comes once in a while and they never know when. It does seem to come when the boss is pleased. So they will want to try to please me, and they do this by working steadily, consistently, well and happily. This they will do not knowing if the bonus will be offered and they do it even when it hasn't been offered. They do so because they never know when it will come, if it will come, but will try for it any time and all the time.

The second thing is I still use the Job Map labor estimate to determine my target final labor price. If the guys are on track enough to finish on time or a little early, I can easily offer them a bonus I would have paid them anyway in salary. On the last day or near the last day I inform them of "the deal". The essence of "the deal" is to finish the job at whatever time of the day and get paid for eight hours. I would feel obliged to pay them for the whole day anyway, but they don't know that. What they do know is they are getting paid for time not worked, and it amounts to a little vacation time. They will even begin a job with the intent of trying to get to a "deal" at the end, but they never really know if they will get it. Sometimes I will offer it, sometimes I will just give it, other times it just isn't mentioned. They never know and must therefore always be on their toes in hopes of getting it.

These "deals" are no-lose situations. It costs me nothing. Even if they take all day, it would cost me exactly the same in salary. The advantage is that I avoid the adrenaline of "will we or won't we finish today?" They feel they're getting away with something, and they have more of the same to look forward to. Win-win!

I realized from the bonus experiments that although money is a powerful reinforcer, there is a limit to how much is too much. I soon realized how this applies to high hourly pay rates as well, where a high hourly wage can grow a guy an undesirably large sense of entitlement.

The rule is an employee must not be paid an amount outside of the expected range. To sweeten an employment deal, individual pay can be a little higher than a guy could expect elsewhere. This can result in his feeling he is doing well, and it doesn't have to cost a lot, with a little more going a long way. All that is needed is for a guy to believe he is doing better where he is than he would do somewhere else.

I also want my employees to feel there is better advancement opportunity for him with me. He must believe he can do better with me. In this vein, I always have one guy whose pay IS exorbitantly high. His pay sets a high bar for the others to shoot for. It acts as a carrot on a stick for them. Although sometimes that top guy will remove the carrot and hit me with the stick.

I have always had a key performer on my crew. There has always been one guy with the longest tenure and the most skills and therefore the highest pay rate. There was one particularly long stretch that ended a few years ago when I had to let go a very valuable twenty-year man.

He had started as the eighteen year old blanked-out know-nothing whom I took under my wing. Through years of my input and his periodic response, he learned the trade pretty well. In fact, his skills in many areas became equal to mine. We worked together as painting peers for many years. There was never any doubt about who was the boss, but he sure knew his way around a paint brush enough to carry his weight and make valuable input. And I encouraged the application of his expertise.

Although he was encouraged to strut his stuff, he went too far with it. When I encouraged him to be the top dog on the crew, he began to swagger. When I set him up to lead the crew, he criticized them mercilessly. When I would leave him in charge while I left to run errands, he eventually would stand around and smoke cigarettes. At one point in his managerial career, when faced with a fellow employee who didn't do as he wanted, he threatened to fight him. And when given raises in pay he began to insist on more. He was the highest paid residential painter's helper in town, but he was resentful. He became unmanageable, disagreeable, and mean-spirited and ultimately was poison to the other crew members. I had to let him go.

The problem stemmed from the amount of money he was paid, that was reasonably based upon the responsibility I placed on him. Together, pay and position ruined him. It swelled his misguided head and he showed his self-centered immaturity. I learned what to avoid.

When he left I elevated guy number two to the number one spot. But I did so with a lot less fanfare, less pay and less authority.

New guy number one never reached the same height of pay, although I could have afforded it and his work could have justified it. I paid him well, setting him up as the carrot on the stick for the others. I used all of the usual bonus incentives to maintain his interest, but was careful about elevating his base pay to ego reaching levels. That kind of glee, I learned, should only be periodically touched by incentive bonuses. And it should never be expected!

I was also careful about his crew status. He was by far the longest tenured worker and most knowledgeable on the various crews during his time, but I was very attentive to his attitudinal messages. In my presence he did not become contrary. The other workers respected him, and that was valuable to him. This became the basis for how I managed him. In a sense, setting him up to receive the respect of the younger crew members was a way for me to manage this new guy number one. In other words, I could arrange for him to receive the behavioral reinforcement he derived from the display of respect from the other guys as a means of my managing his targeted behavior. New guy number one liked the respect he received and wanted to do whatever would bring more of it. I was just careful that he was not free to do much of this by himself for fear of his becoming self-important and independent of me. It was a management device I used to reinforce his desired leadership behavior. He seemed to eat it up.

All things come to an end though and he left me at year ten for a job with a year- round painter. I don't blame and in fact applaud him. Everyone needs to make decisions and changes to advance themself. I'm not the most motivated guy in town. Working only part of the year for me, as my business season offered, didn't pay his bills the entire year. Everyone eventually has to go. That is the failure of my system. But not so for me, for I will always be able to fill a crew, even though it is a whole lot simpler and easier for me when guys come back. And I always encourage them to do so.

In fact, the end of a season is the beginning of the next. Guys who return to work for me are my main asset, so it behooves me to increase the probability of their doing so.

When training animals in a Skinner box, behavior is modified through a process of altering schedules of reinforcement and changing requirements for reinforcement. Technically, it is called changing the *contingencies for reinforcement*.

When guys work for their ordinary, good base hourly rate, and they perform well enough, they will sometimes be offered "a deal". There is no guarantee and there can be no expectation of this. There can be no way for them of knowing when it will come. But as a management tool, that incentive offer becomes an unspoken goal they might earn. So they try for it a lot of the time, because it comes sometimes and not all the time. This is a variable reinforcement schedule.

The ordinary pay is always available, they will always be paid. This is continuous reinforcement, or reinforcement given every time. But that special pay only comes when they are very good in some way. Thus, the contingency, or requirement, for reinforcement in base pay is always the same, but the contingency of reinforcement for the incentive is not quite known, they have to work hard for it, with no promises. The base pay sets up the employee to work, but the possibility of the incentive is what affects their attitude about how he works, how hard he works and to what degree of perfection. In this way, I employ continuous and variable reinforcement schedules, each to control different aspects of desired employee behavior.

At the end of the year, I see to it that each employee has finished with a rate of pay he feels good about. In fact, if a guy is one whom I want to return, I give him a raise, as has been mentioned, a week or two before the end of the season. This is designed to set him up to be most appreciative of his job with me. During an end of year conversation, if he indicates openness to returning I promise him a healthy raise upon returning. I call it a signing bonus, and most, being sport fans, dig the reference. The contingency of reinforcement of the pay increase is MERELY to return. They mostly do. I have had returnees for all of the years I have done this. Of late, I have laid guys off for as much as a half a year. Returning is an easy contingency to meet for pay increase, and they seem to do it.

Managing and motivating guys on a day to day, moment to moment basis is constant work for me. I've met a lot of contractors who just refuse to do it. They say they refuse to baby-sit their guys. I think they view their role as business owner-operator in a different way than I do. They must see themselves as a dictator. They want to give out the orders and then forget about it until the guy is done doing it. I see that management style as lacking the moment by moment attention necessary for dealing with the behavioral management of their help. They abdicate responsibility for their employees' behavior by failing to apply these simple behavior management techniques. I see myself as a continuously ongoing manager- operator-employer. I am a never ending behavior manager.

As a business operator, I am a behavior manager first, a business man second and only then am I a painter. Providing reinforcing events to the desired behavior of my help is what I do. I do it all day long and I never stop. I understand that desired behavior requires strengthening consequences and it is my job to manage guys through my provision of them. This requires constant and frequent monitoring of their behavior as they behave, as they work.

As discussed earlier, I pay them well to promote their feeling good about their job, and I also ensure that they have complete confidence in their being paid every week. Receiving their pay on time and every week is an absolute requirement. Even if I have to borrow the salary money from Visa, I will never allow them to have any doubt about receiving it. I will be so consistent, they will trust me like a grandfather.

If weekly wage is a given necessity, treats during the day are elective. Although they are optional in terms of an employer's obligation to his help, after a while they become not only expected but necessary for morale. I might bring them coffee, cold drinks, donuts or even ice cream or popsicles. These treats are so enjoyable because they tend to come at just those times when they are so damned pleasurable. By managing the occurrence of treats, I can arrange strengthening consequences to appear at the very time when I deem it most effective for reinforcing their desirable behavior. I try to offer them in a way that always promotes desired behavior. And it is highly effective.

I had a tough job going in the brutal heat of summer and guys were grumbling. It is nasty enough working at all in ninety degree heat, but during preparation days of heavy grinding I think they would prefer to be just about anywhere else. It is highly strenuous and dirtier than dirty. And that's not to mention that you can't breathe inside dusty, sweaty dust masks or see through foggy goggles. Inside that heavy get-up it is an all-day exercise class hauling the heavy grinder up and down ladders, and fooling with the extension cords, vacuum hoses, ladders, drop cloths and piles of dust and chips. On this particular day, nobody wanted to be there. It was time for a little contingency management.

In that situation, guys feel like they are on an endless mission. They feel like the grinding will never end and their lives will go on in grinding hell for ever more. At that point I need to supply a *horizon*. Make it to the horizon, I tell them, and there is an oasis. It is technically called contingency management or contingency contracting. I give them a short term goal and offer to supply a reinforcing event at that time. They need to have something to look forward to and it comes in the form of temporary relief from grinding while consuming a drink or some coffee. I ask which they prefer, offer to bring some back after making an errand run and suggest the goal for them to complete while I am gone. Invariably, they come close or meet that goal, and even if they don't, they work hard until I return. I really can ask for no more than that. This is simple contingency contracting. I merely attach the horse to cart, put the carrot in front of the horse and tell it, "go!"

I strategically offer these tangible items, but there are intangible characteristics that guys are seeking that can be given at the right moments as well. Guys want drinks when they're dry and rest when they're tired. They also want recognition for their work, friendship for their "inner selves", membership for their need for community and elderly leadership for their need for male hierarchical bonding. All conditions of relationship can be provided on a strategic basis for the purpose of increasing or decreasing the display of desirable or undesirable behavior. It must be spelled out that although I speak of this as strategic technology, underneath it all is a very high regard for my guys: I really do love them all. But in understanding how behavior works I would be foolish to ignore the drivers of their behavior. Instead, I use what is available to me for the purpose I choose. Why not? These little actions are low hanging fruit and always available.

Ego-wise, we are all in the same boat. We all want to believe that we are seen as being important to the social structure to which we belong. Guys on a painting crew seek this as well, and it can be affirmed by me. When it is affirmed, their behavior that led to that

117

will be strengthened. I can affirm this and it can be strengthened, but it must actually be there for it to work, for it to have any real meaning for him. I can praise him for his carefulness, but if he doesn't actually act that way what good is it? What behavior am I reinforcing?

Most people will have hidden or secret wishes regarding them. These are ego desires they carry that exist within them, almost hidden from expression, all but un-demonstrated in their behavior. Often times others will detect these, but it isn't out in the open for public display. These are inner, personal characteristics the man "wishes" to have known about him, but has difficulty in expressing. When I can detect and then acknowledge this in him, it is a reminder to him what is correct and desirable of him, and it can deeply affirm some essential trait in him. This can act to direct his behavior by providing him with something to shoot for, because he will want to be known for this. Praise and recognition of real aspects of one's personality, those expressed as well as unexpressed, become powerful reinforcers of behavior. It is why intimacy can be managed as a motivator as well.

There was bickering on the crew. So and so thought somebody was a bloody fool. Each nipped at the other's heels and no matter what the other did, it was wrong. I swear they could have been married. I personally didn't care who was right or who was wrong. I didn't care who had stepped on whose toes, I just wanted good work from them.

I separated them, like fighting children, having them work on different sides of the house. After each had begun working well again I took the opportunity to reinforce their desired behavior through the display of my intimacy in offering my trust of them. I asked each of them their account of the problem and what they thought we should do to correct it. I indicated my understanding to each one, accepting how they felt that each was justified and the other's behavior was questionable, being careful to distinguish questionable from guilty. In truth, I had no idea who was what but had a sneaking suspicion they were both being childish. It was no matter, just as the solutions were no matter. All I wanted was to provide a reinforcing event following their display of desired

118

behavior and to increase the probability of their further desired behavior with regards to me and the other guy. Like most spats, this one was no longer visible on the surface, although they never really liked each other.

Moments of intimacy are a manager's reinforcement stock in trade and I offer it as I can to bolster a guy's commitment. Walking around to where he is working I will often stop to chat with him. As long as he is not grinding I can do this while he is working and it becomes a pleasant enough way for us both to spend some time. It isn't as though I dispense intimacy like a can of coke from a machine; I actually do like all of my guys and enjoy talking with them. But I do understand how behavior works and I use that for my purposes. By being on the constant lookout, I can detect those kinds of interactions that serve to increase the occurrence of desired behavior from my guys. This is non-stop work. Because, like the action of gravity, behavioral factors constantly function to control guys' behavior. It is up to me to attempt to manage those factors for my benefit. To not manage them is wasted opportunity and an abdication of responsibility.

There is a behavioral concept called the Premack Principle, coined by a researcher last-named Premack. For some reason he liked the sound of his own name and labeled this behavioral law after himself. He put it like this, but not in these words: if a painter is doing a difficult, undesirable job, he will give it more attention if he knows he will be able to do a "choice" job when he finishes. Technically, Premack put it like so: the display of low probability behavior is increased to high occurrence when the opportunity for engaging in high probability behavior is made contingent upon the display of the low probability one. In others words, when a guy is doing an odious task, I disclose to him his subsequent good luck in being able to do a choice job. This works because a guy has to have something to look forward to.

During preparation, grinding days are everyone's hell. In addition to its being dirty, it is also really, really physically demanding. And in the middle of the dirty, physical hard work, there is a mess of electrical cords, vacuum lines, drop cloths and ladders. And of course there is the dust. And paint chips will be everywhere! Bags and bags of them are hauled off every day. And no one, I repeat no one, enjoys this job. No one enjoys it, but most of my guys, most of the time, tolerate it as necessary for the complete job that only my crew does. They wear it as a tough badge of honor much like the Navy Seals or Army Rangers take pride in their tough regimens.

Sometimes, though, they don't have that bounce in their step and the pride is nowhere to be found. No amount of my cheering makes them feel good about grinding or whatever they're doing. This is when simple contingency contracting can be used to elicit desired behavior by focusing their attention forward, as opposed to the backwards acting traditional reinforcement. I offer them a contingency contract whereby they have something to look forward to that brightens the mood about what they are doing in the moment. In this case, the "horizon" offers a change of pace, not an actual treat. After grinding, for instance, anything is preferable. From the point of view of grinding hell, any other job task is preferable, and offering it as a contingency contract can be motivating enough to help a guy through his grinding hell assignment.

Watching my guys, especially during grinding days, I scan them constantly for the signs of grinding fatigue. They will skip spots in their area, thereby inadequately removing old paint. They will move around too much. I look for the signs of their acting out the growing inner desire to be elsewhere. These tend to be good times to offer a little contingency contracting. Maybe it's an offer of putting on hard to clean, stinky, messy oil based primer, which in that instance is preferable to grinding. In these cases, even the second worst job is better than the worst. It is a way of making even odious tasks desirable.

Attitude rules! When a guy feels good about himself and what he is doing, his job comes out the opposite of how it comes out when he hates what he is doing and wants to be somewhere else and doing something different. I just give him that opportunity, just not in that particular moment. Just do this first and then...

When I was a kid I loved the westerns. There always was a clear-cut good guy and a clear-cut bad guy. They even color coded them to make it easy to know which was which. It's no wonder I use a classic western image in running my business. Essentially, I want my guys to be running their horses and I don't want to see them walking, standing around, smoking cigarettes or leaning against the chuck wagon flirting with the coffee girl. I want my guys to be like the pony express. I want to see them running their horses until they grind to a stop. I want to see them jump off and then on the fresh one riding the hell out, fast.

If I want guys to be making me money, they must be completing items from the Job Map. If they are doing something, anything other than a Job Map line item, they are wasting my time, wasting my money. Therefore, in order for them to maximize the result of their time spent, I strive to eliminate their engaging in extraneous actions. I don't want them doing *anything* that doesn't make me money. Putting out drop cloths doesn't make me money. Mixing paint doesn't make me money. Obtaining tools from the trailer doesn't make me money, nor does cleaning up, setting up, getting coffee or thinking about what to do next. I want them running in a straight line. Set up is necessary and must occur without shortchanging, but it is to be completed with the least amount of salary as possible. I want them up on the horse and riding out fast, the less time they spend saddling up, the better. It is best if the rider is SUPPLIED a saddled horse; at the very least I help him do it.

As the simple behavior manager, I arrange conditions so that my guys will fulfill profit making items from the Job Map. My job is to not only manage their painting behavior, but to maximize the outcome of their time spent.

I do what I must to avoid a time- out where guys engage in non-profit making behavior. If I want them to be running their straight line, I need to clear the path so they can. In this, as much as I can, I eliminate their opportunity to do anything that isn't profit-making. I want to see them run in on their frothing, tired mount, jump off it and onto the fresh one, riding out fast toward the next stop. They should either fulfill a Line Item requirement or go home.

THE CREW, A TRIBE

Guys on the crew are people, too. They are people with personalities and personalities with ego needs. I have ego needs and so do you. I arrange to get my needs met in my business life, but I must assist my guys in getting theirs. Being known for some trait or characteristic is highly empowering for just about anyone. For guys on the crew, it is as powerful as money.

Anthropologists who have studied so-called primitive tribal cultures report observations of tight-knit groups of very happy members. Close and prolonged observation yielded the understanding that having grown up within a tribe, tribes'-people were typically completely known to each other. There were no secrets regarding the personality makeup of any one, and there was commonly observed a high degree of relaxation with each other that stood in clear contrast to the interpersonal distance the researchers found in their own home cultures. In other words, these primitives were happy with themselves and each other in their tribe and that social dynamic was news to the researchers.

Tribal individuals were known to have their specialty talents, and within the tribe everyone knew what these were. So and so is the best hunter. That big guy is a great shot. That woman over there is a wonderful cook. And the feathered guy knows how to assist everyone to reach consensus. People had their specialties, but no one displayed the desire to impress anyone else about it. No one had to "work at" being known for some trait because the person didn't "work at" it, they just "were" as they were. As a consequence, they were known for "how" they were and everyone was known for how they were observed to act. All was out in the open. To act otherwise, to either point out one's own skills or to hide one's own follies, would have been some kind of lie, a subterfuge or egotistical self-serving. That just did not happen.

No distinction was made between what we call positive and negative traits. No behavior was either showcased or hidden. They neither advertised their strengths, nor covered up what they didn't want to be known about themselves. All was visible, without any personal editing. It was finally understood by researchers, that membership in the tribe was defined by this mutual, complete knowing of each other. Members of Western society were known to employ social tricks of self-image making. Typically we hold back, cover up and show off, but not these tribes-people.

In being known completely, a tribes-person established his or her place in the tribe. Tribal membership was defined by being known in this way, and tribal membership was vital to their sense of identity. Being known, then, was a necessary condition for acceptance, intimacy and the definition of themselves. The researchers finally concluded that the condition of complete mutual knowing bred the relaxed demeanor so foreign to their own lives and home societies.

Being known for something is a powerful ego force for moderns as well, including painters. I see it with the guys on my crews. It can drive a person. He will both strive to be known for it and he will be bonded to the group that provides for him to be known. This is truly powerful stuff.

Anyone wants to be known for his positive traits. Anyone would want to be known for being the best worker, the best brush man, the best with customers, the best at picking the winner of the weekend game, for having the best wit or for being the best boss. Negative traits tend to be hidden. A guy will work to cover those up, to avoid being known for them. But if it is truly in the guy's makeup, try as he might it will always come out.

Bob is sloppy. He will become inspired to be neat, but methodical and careful are not his automatic, default nature. It is known on the crew to NEVER work underneath him without an umbrella or even close to him without wearing a haz-mat suit. The fallout from his painting is like visiting Niagara Falls, with paint drips and drops falling like mist and flying off in all directions. He is an excellent painter, if you only look at his work. But his production time always includes cleaning the drop cloths of wet paint, wiping the stuff off the ladder, off the windows and off his shoes before he is allowed to walk on the driveway. This is no secret. He knows he is a walking mess. He is the only guy I have ever known who works in gloves, even in ninety degree heat. He knows he is a mess, usually not just waiting to happen. Everyone else knows it too. He acts as though it isn't that way. He acts as though this doesn't happen.

The first two years he worked for me, his messiness was a subject of derision with the other guys. They snidely criticized him behind his back and treated him like an outcast. Three of them were young, early twenties, and hadn't yet figured out life wasn't just a big unmonitored study hall. They were enormously intolerant and poor Bob had to hide his way of being for fear of receiving their derision. I didn't like it. But democracy won out, and the mob ruled. And Bob remained an outcast with those guys.

In his third year, Bob enjoyed a complete change-over in crew membership. He was the only holdover from the prior two years, and was joined by a totally new guy plus two who reappeared from a few years past. In this new tribe, Bob had the opportunity to find a new level of acceptance.

Having lived through his disagreeable role as outcast at the hands of the immature prior crew, I was careful to at least attempt assisting him to find stature. I would model respectful attitudes towards him for the other crew members to observe. I would speak to the other guys in ways that would promote their respect of Bob. In all of this I followed a simple intent. I wanted to bring his unsightly sloppiness to the fore, but to do it in a respectful way that, although not condoning it or approving it as professional behavior, merely acknowledged it. I accepted it as BEING THERE. I accepted it as something that came out of him, but was not him. He dripped paint like someone might drip sweat. He couldn't help it. I didn't like it, but I accepted it. In time, everyone let the cat out of the bag to acknowledge it in the same way. It was no longer necessary for anyone to hold the fact of his sloppiness in secret, or in derision. Everyone knew this about him. Everyone knew he knew they knew. There was no need for secrecy about it. Eventually, Bob himself came to chuckle about it. But he still wore gloves.

Mark is a hot head. His claim to fame has followed him with trouble no different than stepping in and then tracking dog poop around on his shoe. You remember him screaming, "But he's an asshole!" at the crew picnic on the beach. His hot-headedness got the stuffing knocked out of him there. Then there was his bar fight with the college black belt champion that resulted in his broken jaw and double sized swollen head. Then there was the incident with the policeman, whom he mistook for the stranger he had just beaten up at the county fair. Mark mistakenly punched the cop, and spent the next six months in lockup. And there is an endless list of silly anger moments, like the booting of a five gallon bucket of paint across the customer's garage, or the throwing of a brush-full of paint in a deserving crew-mate's face, or the threat to fight me for failing to display the proper respect for him. He was and is a hot head and it got him in hot water time after time. He has tried to avoid the topic, to overlook his own behavior and to justify it when the topic did come up. Everyone hated him for it.

Throughout Mark's twenty-year history working for me he has walked out and off the job in anger more times than I can remember. He always comes back though, and I have come to expect that he will. He comes back with his tail between his legs, begging me to taken back, vowing to finally, once and for all, curb his anger. I know he won't, but I take him back anyway. I take him back knowing he can't stop it. He knows I know. He knows it too. He knows I know he knows, but he promises.

Why does he return? Why does he grovel before me at that point? He does it because I accept this in him. I don't approve it, condone it or agree with it. I just accept he will do this in his weak moments. It will be a blip on the screen after which he will come back to a "more preferred himself". He will slip out of his Dr. Jekyll to become the Mr. Hyde, only to lose that bad guy to become the good one again. I accept this flaw in him and he knows I do. I am probably the first one in his life to offer him this acceptance, and this fact bonds him to me as if with epoxy glue. By bringing the other crew members onboard with this, he becomes a deep tribal member of the crew along with everyone else who is known for what he does and who he is. Being known in this way paves the way for someone's acceptance within the crew. At that point, his membership in the tribe of the crew becomes a powerful force for his continuing. This is a very useful attitude in an employee.

One day we were all painting together on the side of a house. Bob the slob was there. Mark the hot head was there joined by Cory the scared-y cat who is afraid to go up a ladder. The boss, otherwise known as me, was there, too.

I don't recall how it started, but there is ALWAYS crew banter going on while guys work, and often it is inspired, creative back and forth chatter that really ought to be recorded for radio. On this day something very special developed that was the culmination of a lot of work to bring everyone's foibles out in the open. Someone began to speak about himself, and then it just caught on like wildfire with everyone eagerly joining in to voice their own, previously unmentionable, previously not so secret, personality weaknesses.

Bob joked about his messiness and how HE wouldn't work under himself. Of course Mark tickled us with his ridiculing his own anger and Cory mocked his hefty weight and his dislike of ladders. The boss even chimed in with his constant avoidance of getting his hands dirty, and wasn't it about time for him to go on an estimate or at least go get some coffee? It was a remarkably open session of relaxed acceptance and self-disclosure that would have been the envy of any group therapist. I was proud. I was humbled and I was bonded.

PART4: RELATIONSHIP WITH MYSELF

ZEN OF PAINTING

How small is too little to matter? What does it take to make a difference? A layer of paint is one thousandth of an inch thick, yet a new coat transforms a room. Painting, then, is a minimalist approach to making a difference. But I naturally couldn't care less.

Truth be told, I have never liked to paint and hated it as a kid. I mentioned this earlier, but as a college kid while painting during summers, I counted the days until I would be finished; and when I did, I vowed to never do it again. Some things don't change... Nonetheless I have done it as a business for thirty years, have painted endless hours and days and couldn't have done it without a little psychological inner-work.

Maybe it is just laziness, my inner sloth. But I really don't want to work, accomplish or do. There, I said it! But I have had to work and earn a living, and I have chosen painting to do that. In order to pull this off without feeling like I am in jail, I must engage my mind.

When I do paint I find a way to enjoy it, even though I really do hate it to begin with. What is there to enjoy?

There are certain characteristics of the material, paint, and applying it that I can find particularly appealing. To realize this I focus on the existential moment of painting. Maybe we should consider this the *Zen of painting*. Yeah, I like that!

Paint as a working material is liquid and has a potential for being a real smooth one. The higher the quality of the paint, the more velvety it will be in its liquidity. When I mix it up with a stir stick, I can feel this. When I first dip the stir stick in paint, it is thick and heavy, and it might have a swirly color. When a can is first opened, no paint has the valued silky consistency yet.

I begin by placing the stick into a freshly opened can of paint, allowing it to find its own buoyancy. Maybe it drops to the bottom. Sometimes it floats. This informs me about the "body" of the paint. I form my fingers around the stick and with rounded wrist movements, I swirl the paint in a semi-circle, beginning at twelve o'clock, circling it around to six, seven or maybe as late as eight o'clock. The movement involves lifting the paint as well from the bottom to its top as the stick is moved in its circling maneuver. It is a movement mostly of the wrist, but the shoulder swivels and adds to the lift as well.

At first, I assess the progress visually. But once there is a consistent color to the mix, I proceed to a more tactile judgment. This is a simple, pleasing sensual task. I swirl and swirl until I feel a smooth consistency to the paint. I continue until there is a smoothness that is almost naturally, inherently, unconsciously satisfying to something very basic, very animal in me. On the scale of payment, it is a one dollar payment in a hundred dollar deal, but it is paid in gold. That is how nice it feels! I choose to not be absent to this little treasure.

As I allow myself to feel the appreciation for the smoothness, even the dumb act of mixing paint becomes an act of aestheticism. On the other hand, when I don't take the time to notice what goes on in my hand while stirring, this is merely a dumb act of repetitive motion. I seem to be innately more predisposed to appreciating things. But appreciation does not come reliably on its own. I must remember to look for it.

Rolling paint on a wall can become an act of considerable pleasure, as well. But I don't have that automatically, either. I must look for it. This is also an act of existentially being in the moment to attend to subtle, but real, perceptions of paint application.

I find myself with this consistently smooth, thick, colored liquid that I apply with brush and roller. My aim is to arrange it on the wall, with it evenly spread around and smooth looking. In other words, I try to make it cover and hide, and I put a finish stroke on it to lay it off.

128

Laying paint off is an interesting term. It most likely has no sexual connotation. Although we are talking about the language of tradesmen, so who knows? I am pretty sure it isn't derived from the end of year employee surprise, either. But I do know what it is. It is the procedure for finish stroking the paint on the wall, as a last step in ensuring its smooth, good looks.

Young painters don't do this as intentionally as the older ones do. And they get away with it most, or some of the time. But the practice of laying off the paint is one of the mainstays of the now famous European Method of painting.

In the old days of putting oil based paint on everything, walls as well as trim, it was necessary to give a final piece of procedure in order to make it as nice as possible. When paint is rolled onto the wall and moved around it will undoubtedly be left with topography contours. It will have unevenness, thickness, roller lines, and all of these will still be there even after the painter has worked to achieve a thorough application of the paint in making it cover and hide. After attending to those interim objectives, he must then lay it off to fix it up right. He must give the worked paint a final stoke over the entire area to smooth it and to roll the inevitable orange peel contours in the same direction.

This is the essence of laying off paint but it is no longer necessary with modern paints as it was for the older styled ones. Today's water based wall paints don't show any difference when rolled in different directions. But it does show a difference if it isn't consistently spread on the wall, if there are skips in its coverage or if there are uneven contours from roller lines or periodic uneven thickness. These must be smoothed with a finishing stroke. The result is a smooth, well covered, and consistently colored wall space. If you turn your inner ear to it you will almost hear it whisper sweet nothings to you, "yum". But I have to be receptive to the seduction because I will not hear it unless I am on the lookout for its sweetness.

Brushing paint has its own special pleasures. It begins as an essentially calm act of steady transfer of paint from can to work piece. The preferred conveyance is the brush, but the delivery end of this operation is only limited by a painter's creativity. I can use the brush for this. Sometimes I will use a roller. I have even just poured the paint on to my work. The point is, there is nothing holy about the method of getting the paint out of the can and onto the piece. The only requirements are that there should be no color trail and that the delivery be speedy and on time when you need it.

Once you have stuff on the piece, you have to move it around. Typically, I begin this process by taking a large brush-full of paint and swiping it heavily at the starting point of my work. Then I take a second and do the same a little further along the intended path I will follow on the particular house part. I will continue in this way depositing caches along my future route that I can pick up and use as I get there. In this way I proceed quickly and smoothly along my paint path in spreading the paint somewhat evenly across its intended paint path. Once the paint is spread out I can give it the ol' finish stroke and it is beautiful.

Take special note here. I don't give a damn about painting and wish I would never have to pick up or ever see a brush again as long as I live. But that is just what I start with. By attending to the actual fact of doing it, by noticing the little occurrences of its application, by being present to myself in the moment of painting I can be in touch with the very basic nature of the material and to its application.

Esoteric craft circles refer to this as *making the craft medium one's teacher*. By attending to it, one can learn from it and be guided by it. In this, despite "myself", I can find previously unnoticed, yet appealing, detail in the paint and great pleasure in putting it on. It is up to me. I can choose to remember and look or I can be just as the sloth in me is. It is totally up to me to make the choice.

This is: *The Zen* of painting.

MAKE EVERYONE YOU MEET AND EVERYTHING YOU DO YOUR TEACHER, AND BE A WILLING STUDENT

Here is a universal problem: when you know how to do something. What, you might ask, is the problem with that?

Common wisdom would declare knowing how to do something as the goal of any activity. Even though this is true, it is also a hindrance. Let me explain. Try to understand what will be said as if it were not what you expect to hear. It would be mistaken for the reader to act as though he or she already knows what I mean. As a matter of fact, that would be an example of the case I am making.

Get it?

There is a branch of philosophy called Epistemology. It is the theory of knowledge. It is ironic that they make knowing what knowledge is just a theory. It is in some way, unknowable to know what knowing is. There are only theories about it. Apparently, knowing what "knowing is" is not clear according to the mucky-mucks of philosophy. Let's add to that the operational dimension of knowing, which is knowing how to do something. I submit that the relationship of knowing how to do and actually doing something carries its own problems.

When people go to do something, that is anything that they have experience with, they do so with a sense of what the actions are for the purpose of that activity. You could say they "know" what to do. In this sense, when we go to spread the jelly on the toast, brush the paint on the wall, walk across the floor, anything, there is doing it and there is knowing how to do it.

Have you ever watched someone apply jelly to toast? Or paint to a wall? Jelly or paint will ALWAYS go places not intended for it to go. Would we say these individuals did or did not know how to jelly the toast or brush the wall? We would say they did. So if they did, how come the mess?

Knowing how is not enough when doing an action.

An obscure, early twentieth century scientist, Alfred Korzybski, nailed this concept. He coined this piece of insight: *the map is not the territory.* You might have a map of the area, but that doesn't get you there, it doesn't make you be there. I equate knowing how to do something with being the map, doing it as being the territory. Knowing how to do something is only a starting point. One must engage something else when actually doing the action.

Take the example of spreading jelly on toast. It is a simple task. You take the jelly from the jar on a knife. You hold the knife upright as you transfer it towards the toast, being careful to keep the jelly on top and the knife on the bottom. You push the loaded knife onto the toast, turn it to a forty-five degree angle and happily plow the jelly around the toast. If you happen to look back, there will always be traces of jelly on the side of the jar, on the table, the plate or on the crust of the toast. If one knows how to do this, how can there be so many errors? The answer is simple: knowing is just advice, no more than cheap talk about it. Knowing is merely the map, it is not the territory. How then do we come to the territory? How, exactly, do we do an action with accuracy?

It is easier to see in others, but it is manageable only in one's self. Imagine undertaking carrying a load of groceries from the car to the kitchen. When the bags become heavy you still have to carry them. You don't drop them along the way. We don't tend to treat "doing" with the same respect. We do tend to drop something along the way of "doing" an action. We tend to begin an action with our intent to do it using our knowing how to do it. But if you were to observe yourself clearly, you would notice that almost immediately after beginning an action we forget we are doing it while the relevant body parts finish the action. This is called: *"losing our attention".*

There is usually an auspicious beginning to our actions, full of good intentions and a clear mind that ends up on autopilot with little or no mindfulness. Thus, there is the spilled jelly, there are drops of paint, and there are all the other mistakes and mishaps that accompany most actions from morning to night.

The practice of Zen relates to this, suggesting a very simple, yet not easy answer. It is the practice of attention. A Zen master was asked what the essence of Zen is and he answered that it is attention. When pressed to elaborate a more complete definition than just a one word Zen understatement, the master relented to pronounce the expanded answer, "attention, attention, attention!" Apparently we cannot have too much of that.

This is not arcane, esoteric philosophy, but it is experiential truth. What is being spoken about is that we may know how to do something but we tend to forget we are doing it while doing it. In other words, we go to do an action, and then tend to lose our attention along the way, allowing that action to proceed after just setting it in motion.

We go to jelly the toast but do not carry attention all the way through the action. We know how to do it, right? There seems to be no need to "expend" the attention for that lowly act. But what happens? Jelly winds up where you didn't want it. It does so only because you didn't carry your attention all the way through doing it. To begin the simple act and then to do it WITH ATTENTION, is to bring what the monks call *beginners mind* to jellying the toast. Congratulations, you are now practicing Zen!

As a minor footnote, when speaking to my wife about this she casually informed me of her incredulity. Anybody knows you transfer jelly with a spoon!

Oh, I definitely live in a box of my own making! My insistence to apply jelly with a knife speaks to the issue of my faulty map about handling jelly. I have believed jellying toast is accomplished following a knife delivery system. It becomes news to me that the clean part of the world uses a spoon. Yet I persist with the messy conveyance, never once being able to give up "MY" way of doing it. I cannot give it up even though it doesn't work. I believe it is how you do it, and the dripping jelly is inevitable. This is an inaccurate map.

We undertake the doing of actions with more or less attention, but we also can undertake them with more or less accurate intentions. All of our actions have both of these inherent complications and our tendency is to ignore each of them. We have either inadequate attention or inaccurate maps. And we ignore both possibilities to our own individual misfortune.

In any pursuit, when a person is good at something, he will undoubtedly report he has better days with it and worse ones. Take a golfer. Some days the guy can really hit them, some days he is off his game. Take a major league baseball player. A big time slugger can go through hitting slumps as well as hitting sprees. If you ask either of them what is the difference, invariably they will answer by talking about being in the moment or in the zone, having all the time in the world. He might speak about having an expanded attention in the moment of action. Even a major league slugger has to bring more than knowing how to hitting the ball. He must ATTEND to the task IN THE MOMENT.

Knowing what to do is having a good advisor. But doing is more than taking the advice, it is IT being DONE. Attention to detail, attention to the doing, attention to one's self doing it, all of this is the actual territory. Do we want to avoid the drips, the spills and the usual mishaps and mistakes? Then, it is Attention we must do when we do anything.

Ah! Let's call this painter's mind....

The finisher's attitude, then, is not the only requirement for my painters. They must also have this quality of Zen mind I am calling *painter's mind*. Bob usually lacks it; he is a walking paint bomb. What is *painter's mind*? It is attention to detail with attention for one's self doing it while holding attention to all that surrounds him in the scene in which he is doing it. This is what I strive for in myself and what I assist in my guys. It is Zen mind, painter's mind, the painter's requirement.

STYLE, DISCLOSURE and HONESTY, OH MY!

Ask a business owner what is his or her business, or his or her product, and someone in my industry would answer using the word painting. But is a farmer just a dirt digger? Was Michael Jordan just a basketball player? There is the activity one engages in, and then there is the WAY he does it. In my painting business I have developed my own style. The smart guys these days call it *branding*.

I think it started when someone referred to me as the Mercedes Painter. I liked that! In my third year, I bought a fifteen-year old, but pristine, Mercedes-Benz. I chose it because it had a huge trunk in which I could keep all of my tools and supplies. Close the trunk, and there was no indication of my trade. All was a secret unless I was between jobs, and then this classy ride had a stack of ladders on top, offering as incongruous an image as a nose sticking out from your ear.

I hadn't thought of it as style. I never considered it as image. But I began to be told I had it, as I continued to be called the Mercedes Painter. The more I heard this, the more I enjoyed the status suggested by it. This led to my pursuing this image and the beginning of developing my personal style, the Kliman Painting brand.

Style, reputation, image, personality, brand, character, integrity all deal with an intangible level of doing business. These traits are what animate the dirt digging, the basketball dribbling or the painting into an identity that is more than just digging, dribbling or brushing. I began to consider who it is that I wish to be, or who it is that I wish to be known as. THAT is who it is that I began to be in interfacing with my clients. My style, my image, who it is I like to be known as, became my personal standard. And it came to define for me my identity as the successful painting contractor.

"He who I wished to be with my clients" became my goal, as painting became merely the means to that end. My business-self became less about "what" I did than about "whom" that did it. Not to be seen as a phony manipulation of imaginary self-image, this attention to identity is more a recognition of a serious essential psychological fact. Modern psychology, as well as established systems of esoteric, spiritual and even religious teachings, speak of a person's comprisal of many "selves". In this case I am merely "choosing", or recognizing, who of my many possible personality sides to be. This becomes an act of truly authentic genuineness by choosing carefully, so that what I do actually becomes merely the actions of "he who does it".

In this kind of venture I am not a painter but a businessman, a trader whose wares are labor for pay. And he, in me, who does it most successfully, has a preferred personality and identity. Doing the trade is infinitely easier, greatly facilitated, when I see to it that my customers deal with that preferred side of me. So it is best when I remember that image to both them and me. This acts as a self-perpetuating loop as my drive for my image was reinforced by business success which was itself made possible by the style of myself that did that business.

Have you ever tried walking in deep snow? If it is up to your knees when you step in it, snow travelers call it post-holing. Your legs bury themselves like posts that are being set in the ground. A seasoned winter explorer would no more go out without snowshoes than a painter would try stepping between the rungs on his ladder. Falling in is really not a viable option. Personal style in business is what a business person assumes in order to avoid the pitfalls in his relations with his clients, his money exchangers. It is how he avoids post-holing in the interpersonal issues that will inevitably arise. My style can be summed up as to never have to look over my shoulder. I leave no reason for anyone to sneak up on me for retribution. This is not the case for the business world at large.

Our society is comprised of a lot of different styles and personalities. In fact, as a sign of our times, we become habituated to ways of doing business that maybe would not have flown in prior times.

Who hasn't been subjected to the small print test? Something you buy breaks, you go back for service or warranty, only to be referred to the small print. This is a small print world of fast talking double talkers. Take your mind off the ball and you will lose your money. It only looks like a fast ball; it is really a curve ball. It looks like a good deal, but it involves small print.

There is the offer for no-interest credit cards with no balance transfer fees. You sign up for it, transfer a balance only later to be billed for a one time balance transfer COST. The small print explains the difference between fee and COST.

Perhaps you are one of the ones suckered into one of those advertised car leases. You see on TV that you can have one of those shiny new ones for only $ 199 per month. In these cases it isn't just the small print, it is also the fast! Only briefly does it state the amount due at closing that reduces the monthly payment to that amount. Simple arithmetic would show that if you figure this dollar amount into the monthly payment, you are left with a payment roughly equal to buying the thing. Therefore, there is no great out of pocket advantage to leasing. Like Lucy, they offer the football but pull it away before you get to actually kick it.

Maybe you are one of the gullibles like me, who jumped when they read the ad I saw not long ago. Laptop computers were offered for $ 200. I was at the store within an hour of their opening, either just before or just after you. But neither of us walked out with one because they were sold out, we were told. Maybe it was and maybe it wasn't bait and switch, but when the sales guy lamented they were sold out of them, there I was considering a very expensive one. How about that!

The point of all this is that a certain number of years ago, business practices like these would have earned someone a lynching, a tar and feathering or at least a quick run out of town. But not today! Today all kinds of lies are given with a smile on the face and a pen pushed at you by a hand connected to it. I promise to sell you a failsafe new gadget, guaranteed forever, subject to the conditions on the back, refer to small print to discover a definition of forever, the limit of liability or what is meant by the offer of guarantee.

What a world we live in! It is one in which businesses small-print us into submission but one in which the ingenious try to beat the system. A lifetime smoker sues the tobacco company because of the smoking-related illness he blames on them. The long time drunk smashed up his car and self during a binge and the family sues the bartender. My favorite is the couple who "bought" a co-worker's severed fingertip, and tried suing the restaurant in whose soup they pretended to find it. Talk about pointing a finger!

It is true we live in a world of dog-eat-dog desperation due, in part I am sure, to the intentional deception by which some companies do business. But there needs to be a better solution to lowlife, deliberately misleading customer deception. Taken as a whole, all of these practices smell bad. If it were soup, we would throw it out!

Who would want to do business with someone who lies? The answer is: all of us, apparently. Because that is how business in the twenty-first century is conducted. Nonetheless, I do it differently.

When I approach someone for a sales call they are a prospect, but essentially they are someone who has invited me to their home. I act like a guest. When they hire me, they become a customer. But when I finish, it is a friend who pays me. It is this relationship journey that I foster in my business.

If there is one characteristic of usual sales it is the intensity of the sales pitch. The salesman will pound you with the reasons why his product is best. If he doesn't pound you, he will at any rate talk circles around you, spinning his logic of the superiority of his product. At every turn he will work to convince you why you want to buy his unique thing. Every question you have is covered by his boilerplate blanket and stock answers. You're told what to think, how to think it and why. All of your questions are replaced with their pat answers. And then of course there is always the small print.

In my sales approach I have no pat answers, no boilerplate responses and no small print. I seek a partnership in a potentially mutual project. The first thing I do is look for a basis for a relationship. I remember I am a guest at their home. Although invited, I hope to be asked back and I want it to be voluntary. I don't want to return only because I got them to sign on the bottom line. First I find a basis for establishing trust and from there all can proceed nicely. Without it, I walk away willingly.

I prefer not to sell, but to educate. I find it much easier to have integrity talking about what I know and expect than it is to talk about what someone else should want. This is the honesty factor. As intelligent, high functioning, successful members of society, my customers are usually put at ease by this approach. Absent are all of the usual and expected sales stratagems: there is no come-on, there is no hurry up with a limited time offer, there is no first time discount, there is no multiple discount, there is no two for one double talk, no spring specials and definitely no small print. This is a sales call conducted without selling. I bring no smoke for the eyes or wool to pull over them. This is a sales call absent of sales.

I don't try to sell anything, but instead explain and describe. In this, I am an educator, a role I am comfortable with. As such, I inform them what I will do and why I will do it that way. I explain the possible outcomes of alternative approaches. I describe what they should expect from all of the possibilities and I inform them how much they will have to spend. I never tell them what I think they should do, think or decide. In this way I strive to establish, or hopefully to discover, a relationship atmosphere of mutual trust, with mutual integrity of two peers in a possible communal partnership. My aim is to enter into a relationship with both of us facing a common problem together, as partners, not facing each other as adversaries. I am searching for the mutual trust that is the cooperative foundation for the possibility of willingly exchanging a lot of work for a lot of money. Instead of hurry up and get paid, soured by suspicion and cover-up, I enjoy a mutually satisfying journey of complete disclosure.

I love it when my customers see my job in progress. I can tell them and I can tell them, but when they see it they know. If it is during the preparation stage of the job, they will witness a team of workers strenuously laboring to remove enormous amounts of old paint from their place. For the first time, maybe, they will view the actual wood underneath all of the old layers of paint. If it is during the painting, they will see the great lengths gone to for the purpose of protection. They will see equal care given to the application of the paint and they will see the precision and skill of the applicators. And in all, they will see a team of hard working, steady working, conscientious and dedicated workers who enjoy what they do, enjoy each other and do it all with enthusiasm. And they will be happy to see them working on their house. And did I mention the relief they inevitably display? This is one aspect of my complete self-disclosure. It is always a convincing scene because everyone respects honest, hard work.

The difference between a sales come-on and the real deal is how each stands up. The real deal is what it says. The come-on only says what it is, but saying it doesn't stand by itself. I have developed a style and therefore a reputation of being thorough, careful, hard-working and honest. That is how I want to be known, and it is my goal to use the painting business to attain that. My paint job and the process of doing it walks the walk that I talk. Customers respect that and willingly do business with *he who does that.*

BEWARE THE ONE-WAY MIND

In my annual business schedule, I only work a half year or so. You would think all of my time off would be a dream come true. And it well may be, but dreams are a false reality. As the dream that it is, it always comes to an end, I will have to once again re-create a business and willingly, if reluctantly, enter that world.

When I do, gone will be my relaxation. Gone will be the utter absence of a to-do list, the nowhere-to-be-found feeling of the requirement to have-to-do... anything. During this dream-time there is no thing I must do. As it ends, my six month spending spree also ends and it is time to replenish the cash supply.

I have been at this so long that the normal tendency for the fear and trepidation of temporarily giving up the business in the Fall no longer grabs me by the throat. But like back- alley muggers, these undesirables wait and plot and constantly threaten.

Can you imagine the utter vulnerability of completely, albeit temporarily, cutting loose your entire income source? Hell, it isn't just a vulnerability, it is fiscal suicide! I let the help go some time in the fall and have no guarantee of their return. Maybe I have a job or two waiting until spring, but all winter there is no ring on my business telephone. I don't even check for messages.

My guys are all highly-skilled practitioners of my method. My approach to painting jobs is to bring a well-trained team of self-starting, role playing painters. I can't show up with guys who need to be shown which end of a grinder to hold. My guys need to put their boots on the ground and begin the show. That is what the nice people pay for. But come the typical April first, I have neither cast nor show to put on. And like the receding snows of spring, my personal finances have dwindled to not much left.

In years past, I have run my savings account into the ground, literally! I have run it to zero and then into the red during the long, cold spending spree. My first year painting I miscalculated my winter needs. Even though I was a complete miser in those days, living the meager, granola lifestyle of a former sixties hippy, I ran out of money during the winter. I lived on credit cards and eventually maxed them out. At just the time when the minimum payment was due on the cards with which I had no more credit available, spring work started up to save my sorry little butt. I learned the lesson of squirreling enough way for the entire long winter. And I was hooked on the Jekyll-Hyde lifestyle.

As time went along, I became more comfortable with the process. I began to trust that work will come, even though there was none during the winter and early spring moments. The phone would always eventually ring. The lesson here is that conditions will not always be as they are at any given moment. Buddhists say all of life is impermanent. Apparently this also includes my personal finances.

I used to take ski trips. I loved them, taking as many as three in a given winter. These glory episodes didn't grow on trees! My favorite destination was Taos Ski Valley, staying at a very posh money pit. I wasted the most money on those extravaganzas! I had no business taking those trips, but they were so enriching for me personally and for my wife who discovered her inner artist while shopping in Santa Fe and Taos.

I remember one winter in particular putting the entire cost of that trip on a credit card. Those many thousands of dollars was a major amount of money for me that would take quite a commitment to pay back. But I did, and it worked out. It always works out. Sometimes it doesn't work out like you want, but you continue and it is all right.

There is a common belief that a job is secure, if one has a position in a company he or she is set, safe and secure. Operating a business is absolutely none of that. And in light of our current economic conditions, a job sure isn't either, as it turns out.

Business is objectively a complete unknown. All anyone can count on is what has happened. Thus we have forecasts, indices, graphs plotted with measured performance. In short, these are measures of cumulative and selective business performance history. Consider quarterly and annual federal reports, all business statistics and any discussion of business performance. If they were a sentence, they would all be spoken in the past tense. All of their information is historical, because what happens next can't be said yet. All you can talk about is the past. The future is unknown, what will happen is unknown. As business owners we can count on nothing except the pretend crutch, the fantasy of business forecasts. As business owners, we look forward to an utterly unknown future. The unknown is damned uncomfortable.

My first season I had no idea what to expect, having not done it before, and was blindsided by the end of year death of available work. I ran out of jobs to do. My income ended sometime around Thanksgiving and didn't pick up until sometime in March. I had lived hand to mouth all summer. At that point I helplessly switched to card to mouth, living off plastic lines of credit.

The second year I actually saved some money, after paying off the card debt from the prior winter, but didn't save enough to get through that subsequent winter without going red. It probably took fifteen or so years before I could save enough to avoid going into debt during the winter. I might say I have gotten used to it. But the angst still accompanies these four, five or as many as six month periods of income interruptus, and it is almost ulcerous.

I have always been wound tight as an individual, but never had been an anxious one. But anxiety has become a constant companion, a business partner if you will, who never completely leaves the room. The unknowable future is, in and of itself, unnerving, but my whole life needs to be built upon this unknown. My life, and everyone's I suspect, is a house of cards.

After my first year's comeuppance during the winter, I resolved to make mine a pay as you go economy, quite unlike our current federal fiscal policy. I paid for everything, never using the line of credit. Debt wasn't permitted during the income season, although I knew it would become an inevitable necessity. It frightened me, knowing to my bones the uncertainty of future income. Who knows when the income stream will end or when it would begin again?

With this conservative fiscal policy I was free to buy and spend as much as wanted, just not to borrow to do it. I was terrified of getting hung out to dry in debtors' prison. Shame was lurking just around the corner, poised to strike down on me at a moment's lapse of diligence. I was constantly on edge, worried I might wind up having overlooked a sucker punch from the stark, undeniable truth of my helpless uncertainty. Any little wind of change could knock over my house of cards.

I was afraid to buy a suitable work truck. I was afraid to buy a house, as was I afraid of buying furniture, appliances or anything on credit. And I sure wasn't adding to the bottom line of any future happy retirement. I was just playing fiscal catch up and strove only to pay my own way. Cash was king, and cash ruled my world.

I often walked around with hundreds and sometimes thousands of dollars in my pocket. It gave me a sense of security, arguable a false one. But it was known and tangible and with it in my pocket I had no need to borrow.

As paying my own way became more the norm, Anxiety didn't go away, but we somehow took on a new business partner, Confidence. The new guy was a small minority partner at first, but he made his presence felt. Whereas the old timer, Anxiety, carried his weight with all of the dominance his long tenure in the company would expect, the new guy Confidence spoke in ways almost heretical to Anxiety.

Heresy is not really that far-fetched a characterization of the messages from Confidence. The fear spoken of by Anxiety is so raw, so deep, and so visceral, it occupies a position of desperation and demand in me almost on the level of a revered, unchallengeable religion. Anxiety speaks of the fears of loss, of danger and of shame. And to go against that is like *talking shit to the Pope*. YOU JUST DON'T DO IT!

But this Confidence kid brought some fresh air into the board room of my mind and we started to listen to him. In fact, I liked him and saw a bright future there as the prior conservatism of my- pay- as-

I-went economy expanded to a small, and then larger, debt reliance experiment.

I began to feel confident that as life has gone, it will again. And now it is today, and I feel life is magic. The past is known, the cycle of business has gone on and on so many times that I have to feel it will continue some more.

Now I put my business self to rest in the fall with a degree of comfort. Anxiety still speaks, but Confidence exists now in my emotions and in my bones. It holds sway over the fear that is rightfully there, the fear I have always known as a business man. This is the fear of the unknown, rightful and true if not for the remembering of the success of thirty years, thirty cycles of adequate business income. And in that way, I have rightfully come to count on what has happened to continue.

Anxiety and Confidence eventually came to a mutual understanding and agreed to take on a new partner who came to the door. Thus appeared Patience.

I have always been an impatient person. Maybe it is a male trait, maybe it is just my own personal flaw. But when I go to do something I want to get 'er done! This is not the most conducive attitude for completing a task to perfection or for satisfying customers. A job takes as long as it takes and customers need to feel well taken care of. Neither of these is well served by HURRY UP! RUSH! HURRY!

Elsewhere I speak of my Job Map and how I use it to control production time. In a sense, I can use it to target my profit for a given job. It is quite technical, quite accurate and definitely do-able. But it gives me impatience. Like eating spicy food, the nutrition of the Job Map held too tightly gives me a stomach ache. It produces impatience which leads to anxiety, and that I wish to avoid.

The interesting thing is, the intention of a strictly adhered to Job Map is to make a given amount of money. But as above, life being the magic that it is, the job that proceeds at its own rightful pace makes adequate profit without making it necessary to squeeze more out of it.

Whereas in the past, I used to follow the daily production with one eye and with the other keep track of the time estimates of the Job Map. Nowhere would I allow daily production to vary from the confines of the blueprint of my estimates. At each step of the way I would compare the two and make adjustments to proceeding lines from the Job Map whenever production lagged behind the estimate of prior ones. I was a time- crunching fool who always made it across the finish line at the exact moment forecasted by the Job Map. But it was not without anxiety, it was always full of impatience and its result tended to be compromised by some lapses of quality.

After thirty years of doing it though, I have built a nice reputation and have risen to the top of the local painting industry based on the jobs I do. It is not that I just charge more for the same job as others, but I really do give more. I give an objectively better product and I can get a good buck for it. One of the perks of the elevated cost of my jobs is that I don't have to penny pinch hours from the job. Whereas in the past I controlled production time, I now "point" a guy in a direction and then "pick him up" when he finishes. It takes as long as he takes.

There is an old trade's phrase: *don't do a job to get it done, do it until it is done.* This attitude prescribes a tradesman doing his absolute best, and I adhere to it as much as I can. At the same time, when I am the one handling the paint brush, it only looks as though I am casual; it only appears to happen with aplomb. Nonetheless, whenever one of my painters' production time lags too much from the Job Map they are either pulled from the game or given a new assignment. Income rules, quality only serves that: laissez-faire, but only up to a point.

All things take the time they take to do it. Becoming comfortable with what actually happens is the main part of my job, and it is my Personal Work. It is my Zen. This includes everything that I must do. It serves my growth to become comfortable with that reality. Working in this way I discover a real satisfaction in handling the customers and running the crew. Field General-ing is good stuff! These ancillary aspects of the business are what hold my attention, a possibility completely apart from anything to do with me putting on the paint.

I also continue to look forward to the culture shock of dealing with underachieving, desperately self-protected, but deep down, good guys who work for me. When talking to Mark on the phone the other day, I mistakenly made a comment regarding wishing to avoid hurting a co-workers feelings by not having that one work some days. Mark's response was an expression of derision for that point of view and it was like a slap in the face to me to remember just how hard-nosed these guys are, intolerant, crude even, and therefore requiring toughness from me that I don't completely agree with or like in myself. But it nonetheless remains necessary for me

I know I will become, for the limited period of time of the season, one who can manage these guys. This means I will temporarily become somewhat insensitive in favor of a strongly focused goal orientation. I will pursue that income with a single-minded purpose that just must take precedence over other impulses. I will be tough and hard-nosed, not my nature, in order to handle these wild guys.

Last year my management style went contemporary in its use of humor. But even this became so automatic it ran on its own.

Humor could be used at every step of the way to produce a "ha-ha" when directions, criticisms or any kind of statements were given to one of them. It became automatic to make some kind of lame joke whenever I said something to anyone, crossed paths or spent any amount of time with one. It became so automatic that I was even feeling the impulse and sometimes actually doing it outside the workplace with friends or family. It is alarming to see in myself such high strength automatic reacting.

I look on at people who have a job, a career, or, for God's sake, maybe, a POSITION. People incorporate their professional style, what they learn, practice and then do all the time, into the rest of their lives. It spills over where it was never meant to be. A case can be made for its appropriateness in business. But it winds up being what they give their family and friends.

They don't put it down as I do for months at a time to completely forget it. They don't, in other words, have the chance to restart themselves. They don't reboot. They don't leave it alone for months at a time in order to rediscover their own basic nature, only then to return to the business role for a fresh, second, or thirtieth, chance. They identify with the business selves, become what they have done and, I suspect, do not lose it easily. In my loathing of the necessity of the requirement of being the narrowness of my business self, I shudder at what I would become if for not walking away from it completely for months at a time.

In the main, scarily, I think that many of the powerful business types value who they become in their ongoing and never ceasing practice of power. To learn the skills and inner postures of business and interpersonal power might seem the ultimate goal for many people. But I don't think so, not for me.

Granted, I don't achieve anywhere near the income or power levels of CEOs and big business managers, but I experience all of the qualities on my scale.

As business owner, I have an increase in efficiency, power, authority, interpersonal ability and money. I have these things in ways that are beyond my usual or expected levels, and these traits become strong to the point of existing and occurring on their own. It is with the degree of automatic functioning that I have the problem. I am speaking of the fact that my personality seems to adjust to include these behaviors even when outside of the business place. What one does repeatedly becomes how one acts often. The more one acts in a given way, the more identified does he become with that way of being. Repetition doesn't make it any more genuine. Think about it!

It is in just this way that a person can become their functioning, losing in that process their basic, personal human qualities. In the pursuit of the bottom line and in getting others to accomplish it at all costs, one is for better or worse, changed. And out the door are basic human values like caring, sensitivity, helping, positivism towards others, compassion, empathy and many other traits that we all admire in others and love in our selves. And did I mention forgiveness?

The constant unrelenting-ness of a fifty week a year POSITION requires a person repeating the business/ management-necessary interpersonal skills. In time, the repetition drives away the finer traits replacing them with the efficient and domineering ones. At some point, these bottom-line traits take over and define the person. The person becomes those traits and it is just who they are. No more Michael or whoever.

Now he is known by others, *and especially by himself*, as he who does these kinds of things and thinks these kinds of thoughts, acts a characteristic way using a particular outlook and expectation of others, and sees and uses others only in terms of their fulfilling his particular needs. And when I meet people who are so defined in these ways I am not only mightily unimpressed, but appalled by *the power of the unrelenting-ness of their One-Way Mind.*

NOT ONE, BUT AT LEAST TWO

My annual winter free time is the defining perk to my business and personal life. In a nutshell, the time off, and no doubt the grand amount of it, affords me the full opportunity to completely relax. There is relaxation, and there is relaxation. When I say I relax during my winter of Saturdays, I am not saying I let my hair down, whoop-it-up or curl up with a book in front of the fire. I am not talking about taking time out from my busy and intense business schedule to enjoy the good things in life or that I goof-off. I am talking about relaxing into a completely different me. I am talking about a complete and essential transformation of myself. Literally, I become someone else during this time. And NO! I am not schizo. I am just relieved.

In hard-core esoteric and/or Zen circles, there is discussion of the human condition of the individual as being comprised of many "selves". A person is understood to be conditioned to identify him or herself with any of his or her many different personalities or selves. And that the goal of self-realization or enlightenment has to do with discovering, in the midst of all that presumed identity, one's true self. My long winter's respite from life's compelling demands allows me to shed its ever present grip. During the course of these many months of purely self-driven pursuits, slowly I move toward a condition of self largely absent of the need to compete with or accommodate the world. Eventually I become, in the words of a close friend, Winter Michael.

Winter Michael is relaxed. He sleeps well, as opposed to his business-cycle rendition. He will mostly sleep an entire, uninterrupted night of seven or eight hours with the occasional ten hour lay-about. He often doesn't know what day it is. His concern lends Itself to the question of what to eat and whether, and more likely when, to go skiing. Writing is possible, when during the business cycle it is not, because in the winter's relief from schedules and daily minimums there isn't a more prevailing life requirement that must be done. There is no job to do, business to run, employee issue to iron out, or customer angst to sooth. There is no demand written into the play of my winter-time, and I am left free to improvise. The stage becomes set for an exploration of the subtlety and nuance of my best understanding in the observations I make of my life. I am then a different guy, one who only shares the same body as the business self. These two are different people, not the same at all, with entirely different skills, values and outlooks. When one is present the other is clearly not.

Transition from business to freedom is a gradual process. When I cease working for the season, I no longer go to sleep or awake with the intention of going to work, thus my Winter of Saturdays. But my *self* takes time to adjust to the absence of the need. It takes upwards of a month to shed that expectation. Normally in my business self, no matter what I do, there is the expectation of a boogey-man, in the form of an employee, a customer or some other business concern, to jump out from around the next corner to "Boo !" me. Little by little that next corner gets pushed further and further away until it isn't there anymore. And in this way, the impulse to be on guard and vigilant disappears. As I said, essentially I become a different person. Like a glacier receding in the cycle of a warming earth, all of my business impulses, management expectations and on-guard general angst all recede in the relief afforded by the absence of the need to do business.

This is a very complete transformation. Winter Michael knows about Business Mike, but he is a different person. For example, as a hedge against losing favor with my suppliers, I make periodic visits to the stores during the off season. These are not the visits of ease as they would be during the painting season. Invariably, Winter Michael has to "get into" the role of Business Mike. Winter Michael doesn't know how to talk to the paint store salesmen, because his life and world has not a thing to do with business, painting or schmoozing the business contacts. Literally, as Winter Michael, I don't have the understanding to relate to them. The necessary outlook is held in another department of myself, and I can easily understand that "that staff" (of me) is on vacation. Therefore, I have to fake it, and I must somehow simulate, for the length of that visit, the behavior of that part of me. It is not the case that I should be able to be just as I am, as Winter Michael. That is an error of assumption of new-age fantasy. It is the case however, that the paint store guys expect a certain personality when I show up, and that their relationship with me is served by my successful display of that business role. In order to keep them on my side I must ensure that that is who they meet when I show up.

To give them someone else would detract from their expectations and conflict with their comfort level with me. I cannot allow that, and am therefore pressed to only present to them him, in me, who can relate to them. And since "he" is not present, I must somehow manufacture a reasonable facsimile. But as the director of the play of my life, I know that the stand-in does a poor job of portraying Business Mike. The stand-in is not him. He does not have the requisite skills, values and outlooks. But he suffices, and is always relieved to leave the store to end the charade.

Winter Michael doesn't know how to interact with people for profit. As him, I concern myself with interacting with myself for inner profit. I follow a very natural life-style. It centers on eating, warmth, sleep and personal pursuit. At our winter house of retreat in the mountains I follow the gentle discipline of winter hermit-ing consisting of sleeping late, reading, writing, skiing and long leisurely dinners. But that is even a different story. Suffice it to say, Winter Michael has no outside influence, is not driven by outside forces.

The freedom from outside forces permits a whispering voice of intelligence to be heard. Subsequently, I will find myself in pursuit of impulses of more intelligent, more subtle, more valuable and/or soulful meaning. If my mind and heart can be considered filtering systems of awareness, they become extremely fine. I enter a world of ever more subtle and nuanced value and meaning, and my "self" becomes one of ever more compatibility in handling such issues. But woe to fine-ness charged with the coarse! Come spring-time I must re-transform, and it is a shock too much to bear.

It is too much for Winter Michael. That is why he must leave for the re-appearance of the business self. It is always a shock and never what I want. And it always involves grieving the death, the end of my relief from the requirement of satisfying others.

The first sign of "this" spring is my need to make some money. I have been on a five or six month spending spree and I finally allow that it is time to end the bleeding. All winter I know, in the back of my mind, that the only arithmetic activity of my bank account is subtraction. But I don't think about it, I don't entertain its meaning, I don't allow it in my active mind. But come spring, I open the windows of said mind and this compelling fact comes blowing in: "DAMN, I NEED MONEY!"

This is my thirtieth year of this silly painting gig and I can clearly see I will reach retirement with a paint brush in my hand. I become accustomed to what will happen and what does happen. The phone has always rung, and presumably will continue, even though the answering machine has registered a big Zero for incoming calls all winter. Knowing what has happened contributes to a sense of forecasting the future, but I know that is not a certainty. And so, for the thirtieth time, I am on edge and nervous about the upcoming business season.

It is the end of March and where are the phone calls? I have composed and sent out my annual spring mailer to my client list. I have made several trips to my main suppliers to put out the word that I am back. I have called all of my customers who had indicated their intention to have some interior painting done in the spring. But still, nothing.

My thought turns to money. My financial sense tells me that I need a given amount of money to live for a year. I calculate how much I will need to supplement my bank account to make it through another year. My thinking is that if this is the year that proves itself bad, next year will hopefully be a normal one. So I must earn enough to make it through this one to get to next.

My first monetary goal of the season is to have enough work to earn that amount of money if I worked alone. If times were bad and I actually had so little work, I could always just do it myself. With no employee salary overhead I would need far less work to arrive at my magic number. So when I have THAT amount of work, I begin to relax. And it always happens.

At that point and beyond, I know it is safe and prudent to have employees. With more than enough work it is a question of how many employees should I have. The issue becomes less of WHETHER I will make enough this year and more of HOW MUCH can I make and how many guys can I keep profitably busy with the amount of work I will have. Business Mike is back, he knows how to handle it.

Just like that, Winter Michael has left the building.

MY WINTER OF SATURDAYS

Other than in times of crises, we tend to not question "Who am I?" By middle age, most of us, the mentally balanced anyway, have established enough personal routines to make up a whole day. Strings of days make up weeks, months, years, careers and then whole lives. We struggle, enjoy, fail, succeed, plan and improvise through the structure of our lives that we have built and we call this living a life.

The strength of our individual routines has the effect of gravity on our personalities, its influence upon us is total and without interruption. It defines the course of our days and lives just as the highways prescribe where we drive. We so abide by the paths of our routines, that we define ourselves by them.

I have a business to run. The demands are ongoing, continuous and demanding. To do it well, I must do all of the things that make it successful. There is no question of the requirements and there is no question of whether I'll do it.

From Monday morning at 7AM until Friday at 6PM and more likely some time on Saturday, the question of who I am is pretty much taken care of. I am the businessman. By this reckoning, I only have the balance of Saturday and all day Sunday to figure out. And there usually is something that must be accomplished, so I don't have to question about myself much then either.

At this point, it begins to become clear that the question of who I am is more or less satisfied by having something to do. And like the action of gravity on everything in the world, having things to accomplish serves up the stage, the whole play of "Who I am " complete with characters, sets and plot. The more consistently an activity requires doing, the more defined does one become in one's self as the one who does that, as being the person who operates in that kind of play. In this fashion do we become who we are: I am who it is that acts like me in these situations.

Who in this time of American life has not uttered one of the clichés regarding the busy-ness of life? Who hasn't felt the crunch of time to get things done? Who isn't under the gun to accomplish all of the requirements of their life structure? Our to-do lists are filled with what it is each of us must do. Herein does each of us find the blueprint of who we are. Our busy lives define all that we do, all that we know how to do, and therein do we know our selves.

In the familiarity enjoyed with the repeated behaviors and routines do we become who we are. The successful businessman learns his skills of personnel management and bottom-line mentality, and after so many years of practice this poor schlep can no more put this aside than he can his left hand! He never forgets to be the businessman everywhere he goes and in everything he does. There is no questioning of *who he is*, because he is always being that same person. He may take a vacation, but it is the rare individual who can stop being who he is, able to take a vacation from being himself! Behavior learned, practiced and ingrained, becomes the unquestioning modus operandi, i.e. the person him- or her-self!

I have always admired hobos. In my imagination I have elevated them to some enlightened status. I have seen them as social observers, as detached and innocent-minded, and as observant bystanders to the insanely busy pace of our contemporary lives.

Mostly I have coveted their lack of responsibility, their perceived empty to-do list. Who knows their degree of enlightenment? These guys don't have to do anything! They don't have to jump up from bed at some forced and unnatural time to rush out to push themselves to accomplish their daily minimum. They're not bound by an imposed schedule of have-to activities. But they are free, I have imagined, to follow other influences.

Perhaps their sense of self is free-er to some degree. Although, I am sure the individual hobo you would interview would probably fall short on anyone's scale of enlightened personality traits, for the hobo is typically a poor slob who can't stop being a hobo. He, or she, can't stop being the one who is the hobo. He, or she, is defined by all of the behaviors and routines that make up their individual lives. In this, the hobo is no different from the businessman. He is no different, just not the same…

I run a business and subsequently know all about him, in me, who is the businessman. It is a successful business in which I work hard and do well enough financially. It seems I am at or near the top of my profession in the quality of product and in the quality of client. I have much to do to keep it running well, smoothly and successfully. There is no lack of what needs to get done and therefore I always have behavior and routines to do in which I feel myself, in which I identify myself. I have had ample opportunity to learn, practice and allow to become ingrained all of these behaviors and this has become very familiar in me. I know who I am, and I am he who does these things.

But if I *am he who* does these things, who *am I* when I have not these things to do? I am not talking about death, business failure, or divorce, or any other known catastrophe. But in my normal fiscal routine I face this question every winter. Into my off season I take an empty to-do list, and am thereby free. I am free to be *he who is not me*. I am free from the business-cycle required routines.

Mine is a seasonal business, and therefore a part-time identity. While doing business in the course of my business season, I am "he who does business". But at the close of the business season and for the course of a whole winter, I am not that person at all.

On the one hand, my life sets the stage for the businessman and I play that part. All of the behaviors are well established and so is the character. I know who I am and am comfortable with him in that context. But when the painting season recess bell rings, the structure of the business life disappears like some real-life Brigadoon. The known routines are gone and the to-do list is re-issued with a clean slate. And like my fantasy hobo, I have nothing I have to do.

For six or eight months I follow my business regimen like a goose -stepping business Nazi. I would no more ignore my routine than a gay, Jewish-gypsy jail keeper at Auschwitz. I follow the pass route of my business play like a Heisman Trophy candidate on national TV. There is no question, no hesitation and there is no deviation in what I do, the way I do it and who I am who does it.

But in the off season there is no jail to keep. There is no play called, let alone a pass route. I like my to-do list empty because I relish who I am with nothing to do. I like having nothing I must do; it gives me my true purpose, the purpose of discovering who, in truth, I am when there is no need to do something in particular. Aside from all that I must do in life, aside from all of the requirements of my life, what is the true nature of my *self*? Who am I when there is nothing I have to do? I'm told this is an ancient question, the essence of Zen, religion and serious meditation.

I have nothing I must do and my life naturally presents this question, in earnest, during my Winter of Saturdays.